THE TOWNS AND ...
OF SNOWDONIA

The Towns and Villages of Snowdonia

Dewi Roberts

Text:Dewi Roberts

ISBN: 1-84527-028-2

Cover design: Sian Parri

Published in 2006
by Gwasg Carreg Gwalch,
12 Iard yr Orsaf, Llanrwst, Wales LL26 0EH
℡ 01492 642031   2 01492 641502
✆ books@carreg-gwalch.co.uk   Website: www.carreg-gwalch.co.uk

Contents

Snowdonia National Park

This was the fortress of all ancient dreams,
Where princes played, with kingdoms for the stake,
At games of hazard, pledging pass and lake
With Norman brokers; when they lost, it seems,
Their creditors annexed the pawned estate,
And as new landlords proved a greater ill
Since lawlessness could best their coffers fill;
Always were blood and death sad Gwynedd's fate.
It has not changed; still the dark legends cling
To moor and mountain in the ravished land;
In the broad plain Rhiannon's birds still sing,
And nameless lords lie slaughtered close at hand.
Is this your park? Indeed a fitting name
With which to mark a land of this red fame!

Sally Roberts Jones

Introduction

It is surely the hills and mountains which come most vividly to mind when we consider the geographical terrain of the area encompassed by the Snowdonia National Park. Indeed, the writer, Walter Allen, once described it as 'one of the most beautiful parts of the Western world'.

The Snowdon massif, Cader Idris and the Migneint and Rhinog hills combine to make the region unique in topographical terms. It is also one that falls within what is frequently referred to as the Welsh heartland, for the language remains vital and vibrant in the life and culture of Gwynedd and Conwy.

But what of the towns and villages within the National Park? Many of these are steeped in history, as one would expect, and although I am by no means a professional historian, I have spent some time unearthing some of the interesting facets of what has been written about these communities.

Every Welsh town or village appears to have its own enthusiastic local historian working energetically and conscientiously on research into life in the past. The published fruits of their research are invaluable to our understanding of the influences, which have shaped the social and cultural life of these communities. I am certainly aware of my indebtedness to them in my search for information for this book.

In these pages the reader will learn, for example, of Abraham Lincoln's ancestral link with Ysbyty Ifan, of the Irish rebels who were imprisoned in the Bala area following the 1916 Easter Rising in Dublin, obtain an insight into Vosper's famous painting 'Salem' and read a first hand account of the disaster which occurred at Dolgarrog in 1925.

I hope that in its very modest way this publication may encourage readers to seek more detailed accounts relating to the abundantly rich historical association of Snowdonian communities.

Dewi Roberts

Aberdyfi

Cantre'r Gwaelod

When we think of Aberdyfi the song 'The Bells of Aberdovey' immediately comes to mind. Even people who have never visited this part of Wales may be familiar with this melody. It has, over the years been assumed that it was the work of the English composer, Charles Dibdin (1745-1814), and indeed *The Oxford Companion to Music* is unequivocal on this point. However, *The Oxford Companion to the Literature of Wales* claims that 'Clychau Aberdyfi' was first published in a Welsh collection by Maria Jane Williams (1795-1873). The entry states that:

> because the tune had appeared in several English collections before 1844, it has been wrongly described as being of English derivation and ascribed to Charles Dibdin.

The song is thought to have its origins in the legend of Cantre'r Gwaelod or the 'lowland hundred', land submerged under Cardigan Bay between Aberdyfi and Harlech. Was this a legend of folk-memory that had its origins in the Neolithic or Iron Age? Historians have always considered this as a possibility in what is a highly complex area of early history. There is, for example, more than one version of the events, which may or may not have occurred and the one which seems to have the most popular currency resembles similar mythology from other parts of the western world, including the Low Countries.

There were, it seems, sixteen cities which were situated on low-lying ground within an embankment.

Seithennyn was appointed as the keeper of the dyke and it was his job to ensure that the kingdom was safe at all times from the dangers of the sea. Despite the fact that he was aware that the embankment was vulnerable at certain points he failed to alert the king of this. Seithennyn's liking for strong drink did not help things and, one day, when he was in an inebriated state the sea wall broke and the entire kingdom was quickly flooded. The only survivor was the king.

It is claimed by romantics that the bells of Cantre'r Gwaelod can still be heard from far below the waters of Bae Ceredigion (Ceredigion Bay) on calm evenings.

The myths of drowned communities have a particular resonance in northern Wales where the flooding of Capel Celyn and the surrounding valley was carried out despite the unified opposition of various pressure groups. Tryweryn has become a historical cause célèbre.

A Meeting Place for Welsh Leaders

Landscape and history frequently merge in Wales and never more so than on the banks of the Dyfi. It was an important boundary where, in mediaeval times, three kingdoms converged – Gwynedd, Powys and Y Deheubarth. As a result, it became a place where leaders from throughout Wales would come together in order to air their opinions on issues affecting the nation.

Maelgwn Gwynedd called a meeting on its banks to which he had invited leaders from throughout the country. He wished to settle once and for all the matter of who should be the undisputed Welsh leader or high king. It was eventually agreed that this could best be settled by a test of bravery. Each of the leaders from the various regions of the country was asked to bring his throne, and when the tide was low to place it on the beach, which has been known ever since as Traeth Maelgwn. With the turn of the tide, the last leader to vacate his throne, as the water rose around him would be deemed to be sufficiently brave to become the national leader. As one would expect the leaders were far from poor and brought with them some very expensive gilded thrones decorated with gold. Maelgwn's throne however was much more modest and was held together with wax, the seat consisting of goose feathers. As a result, he floated calmly on the tide while his rivals panicked and made for the shore. So the kingdom of Gwynedd led the rest of Wales and made it independent and strong.

When the Normans were increasing their hold on Wales,

Llywelyn Fawr of Gwynedd resisted their attempts to govern the country for their own ends. He called all the Welsh lords together on the banks of the Dyfi and this meeting resulted in the Treaty of Aberdyfi which, quite apart from anything else, consolidated his position as leader. As Beverley Smith wrote, it ensured that ' . . . the leader would be lord and the allies would be subjects'.

The area figures prominently in the life of Owain Glyndŵr. Ships from France, Spain and Scotland arrived, the passengers being ambassadors of their respective kings. The reason for their visit was to be present at the first meeting of Owain Glyndŵr's Parliament in Machynlleth. They had come to witness the leader proclaimed the 'Prince of the Nation'.

It is not perhaps generally known that Aberdyfi once had a castle, albeit a small one. However, it seems that it only stood for six years and was a motte and bailey structure built in approximately 1151 by Rhys, the son of Gruffudd, the Lord of Deheubarth. It had occupied a prominent position on the hill known as Pen y Bryn and was destroyed by the Norman Lord, Robert de Clare in 1157.

The importance of Aberdyfi's coastal position has dominated its history over the centuries since the Norman invasion or indeed the age of Glyndŵr. In the Middle Ages a ferry crossed the estuary according to some sources.

Maritime Trade

In the nineteenth century life in this community revolved around trading. It was a port and it handled a considerable amount of trade along the Meirionnydd coast. Here coal, limestone, bricks and timber, among other commodities, were imported, while exports included timber poles for collieries, lead ore and slate.

Eagle House, situated close to the church, was previously the customs house and, as such, was the residence of Lewis Morris, the eldest of the four remarkable Morris brothers of Ynys Môn. He was something of a polymath – a mining engineer, maritime surveyor, poet, scholar and musician. He was commissioned to compile a survey of the Welsh ports in the years 1755-1756 and during this period was customs officer at Aberdyfi.

By 1880 there were so many foreign ships entering the port from far-flung corners of the world that a navigational aid was erected on the hill known as Pen-y-Bwlch. This proved invaluable, but the days of sailing trade vessels around the smaller ports of Wales were numbered when the railway companies constructed new lines and sailing ships were soon replaced by the steam engines. The railway also made the possibility of holidays more accessible and small coastal communities proved to be very desirable destinies for those who spent most of their working lives in an urban environment. Yachts, pleasure boats and small vessels of other kinds now predominate at Aberdyfi. A lifeboat station with an excellent record had also been built.

1892 saw the formation of the Aberdyfi Golf Club and it was here that the first game to be played in Wales took place. This was in 1895. In 1908 the Clubhouse caught fire. Following the 1914-1918 war the course was much improved and has since hosted a number of important championships.

This is not the only first for Aberdyfi. The first Outward Bound Centre was established in the town in 1941 and organised a wide range of outdoor activities.

World War II

In 1942 Winston Churchill authorised the establishment of a unit of commandos made up entirely of the loyal refugees who had arrived in Britain before the outbreak of the 1939-1945 war. These included Germans, Austrians and other Europeans. In a period of political tension between Germany, Britain and France, these immigrants were anxious to contribute all they could to the British cause in the war effort.

Three hundred and fifty of these men made up a new commando unit, 3 Troop 10. Major Hilton-Jones from Caernarfon commanded them. The training took place in Aberdyfi and they were billeted with local families. The rigorous exercises in the hills of northwest Wales stood them in good stead when they were sent out on secret missions to France in order to contact agents and gather information. But, alas, not all of them were successful for some perished on D-Day and by the spring of 1945 one in four of these courageous combatants was dead. A plaque commemorates them at Aberdyfi and Brian Grant, one of the survivors, spoke on behalf of so many when he said:

> We regard Aberdyfi as the place of our rebirth. After years of discrimination, persecution and second-class citizenship, members of 3 Troop enabled us to participate fully in the defeat of Hitler and to establish ourselves in the post-war world as equal naturalised citizens of the Free World.

The late Hugh M. Lewis, who was an authority on the history of the community, recalls a Welsh childhood which is a refreshingly far cry from the lives of many children today:

> We played endless games with toy soldiers. These were an echo of the military activity during 1914-1918 war and we could base our games on what we heard. Boyhood games could be boisterous, sometimes unruly and occasionally could lead to trouble with the village policeman. However, he was wise to many of our tricks and he had no difficulty in keeping us in order. Sometimes the punishment was on the spot and immediate, such as a ban from the area, a clip on the ears, a threat to tell parents or the confiscation of a possession.
>
> Discipline was strict and moral guidance readily passed on and instilled in us. We were brought up to be dutiful and obedient, to be trustworthy and honest whilst showing respect to our elders and courtesy to all around. We had no doubts as to what was acceptable or unacceptable. Parental decisions brooked no argument and any potential disobedience was immediately checked and suggestions of defiance or insolence were instantly reprimanded.
>
> It was rare for parents to fail in such matters but if they did, problems in families often appeared later in life in some form. Of course, we sometimes resented the discipline as young people will always try to test a system but we invariably respected the disciplinarian and doubted those who wanted to disobey.

No child that I knew grew up with a police record. Violence and crime were practically non-existent and still had the power to shock and horrify. Dad was our family disciplinarian and when he was around we had to be on our best behaviour. He kept a small cane on top of the mantelpiece and if he had cause to speak more than once, a quick glance up at the mantelpiece with the enquiry, 'Where is the cane?' brought about the desired effect. There was never any need to bring it down.

Telephones were scarce in the village and public call boxes completely lacking. If a telephone was needed, which was not often, then a visit had to be made to the village Post Office.

Outside normal hours you had to knock at the door of the postmistress's private flat above the office. Messages were conveyed to residents in the locality by children who received a penny for their services. When a telegram had to be delivered, the postmistress opened the office and blew a whistle. The first child to answer the summons got the job and there was much competition. Serious messages relating to deaths and accidents at sea or in foreign parts were taken personally by the postmistress, who very tactfully broke the news herself before handing over the cold missive.

Further Reading:
D.W. Morgan: *Brief Glory* (out of print)
Hugh M. Lewis: *Aberdyfi: The Past Recalled* (Y Lolfa, 2001)

Bala

Tomen y Bala

Our knowledge of the medieval history of the town is fairly sparse. However, we do know that Roger de Mortimer established the community in 1310. He hoped that by doing so he might be better placed to bring a sense of order to the rebellious Penllyn district where there was a fortification which had been captured by Llywelyn ap Iorwerth (Llywelyn Fawr, the Great) in 1202.

Bala became a royal demesne at a later stage of its early history and fifty three burgage plots were set out in 1310. In 1324 the town was granted a charter and as a borough was able to hold weekly markets and two annual fairs. When it assumed a higher profile as a community, Llanfair, an earlier settlement, situated a mile away, declined in importance.

The pattern of the streets has evolved partly as a result of a Roman road, which existed during their period of frontier rule, while the mediaeval 'back lanes' are parallel to the High Street.

There are remains of a Norman motte known as Tomen y Bala and from the summit visitors can gaze down on Llyn Tegid.

Llywelyn Fawr could well have erected this fortification in 1202, although one has to be careful not to be too categorical about this, for, as with so many distant historical events, reality and myth tend sometimes to be intermingled.

Llyn Tegid

Although the town itself is not located within the National Park, its lake is. Llyn Tegid is almost four miles in length and its maximum depth is one hundred and thirty six feet. There is a legend associated with the lake, which, although well known, still merits repetition.

It is said that a villainous prince was celebrating the arrival of a newborn son and heir. In the midst of all the singing and dancing, his harpist heard a sinister voice above the merriment. It said: 'Vengeance will come'. When he tried to decide where the voice had come from, he saw only a small bird and felt impelled to follow it. The bird took him many miles through unknown country and the harpist suddenly felt he wanted to return to the palace. The following day he reached his destination and to his consternation saw that a lake covered the entire area where the palace had once stood. In the centre of Llyn Tegid floated his beloved harp.

Llyn Tegid is home to a small white fish, the 'gwyniad', which is unique to the lake. It does not seem to be the object of fishermen's desire nowadays, although many travellers who visited Bala in the eighteenth and nineteenth centuries mentioned it. As far back as 1584 we find Humphrey Llwyd writing of 'a kind of fish called Gwyniad which are like whitings'.

The grayling is another fish, which seems to be unique to Bala. When he visited in 1756 Lord Lyttleton was more interested in the women of the area.

> What Bala is most famous for is the beauty of its women and indeed I saw there some of the prettiest women I ever beheld.

A Breakfast to Remember

George Borrow came in 1854, but it was the food, which held the greatest appeal for him, and he itemised the ingredients, which made up a breakfast, which he consumed at the White Lion Hotel.

> What a breakfast! Pot of hare; ditto of trout; pot of prepared shrimps; dish of plain shrimps; tin of sardines; beautiful beef steak; eggs, muffin; large loaf, and butter, not forgetting capital tea. There's a breakfast for you!

The community was well known for its knitted garments. In his *Topographical Dictionary of Wales* 1838, Samuel Lewis writes:

There are two factories for carding wool, and Bala and its neighbourhood have for a long series of years been noted for the knitting of woollen stockings, socks, and gloves, but this manufacturer has of late been on the decline: in the year 1830, thirty-two thousand dozen pairs of stockings, ten thousand dozen pairs of socks, and five thousand five hundred dozen pairs of gloves were made. The hosiery is distinguished for the softness of its texture, which causes it to be held in high esteem for winter wear, and universally recommended by the medical faculty.

By the mid-nineteenth century there had been a decline in demand for the products and trade declined.

Welsh Methodism

The importance of Bala in the religious life of Wales cannot be overemphasised. It was a focal point for Methodism and will forever be associated with Thomas Charles (1755-1814) whose statue can be found close to Capel Tegid. It was through his passionate concern for the peasantry that he was able to organise Sunday Schools and circulating schools. The story of Mary Jones's mountain walk from Llanfihangel-y-Pennant to Bala to obtain a Bible from Charles is, in a religious context, one of the most enduring anecdotes. The visit of Mary made Charles realise that there was a universal yearning for the Christian message and he played his part in establishing the British and Foreign Bible Society which went some way to fulfilling this need. Lewis Edwards, Charles' grandson, founded the Bala Calvinistic Methodist Society many years after Thomas Charles' death.

Welsh Liberalism and Radicalism

In the world of politics, T.E. Ellis (1859-1899) was elected Liberal Member of Parliament for Meirionnydd when Gladstone was Prime Minister.

One of Ellis's objectives was home rule for Wales. He also

threw his weight behind the disestablishment of the Church in Wales as well as the enhancement of educational standards. A cultured man, he has been described as 'the most potent symbol of Welsh aspirations'. Goscombe John's statue of him stands on the High Street. It bears Ellis's favourite quotation, which comes from the pen of Morgan Llwyd:

> A man's time is his inheritance, and woe to him who wastes it.

The man who provided the inspiration for the founding of the Welsh colony in Patagonia was born in the Bala area. Michael D. Jones emigrated to America in 1847 when he was the founder of the Brython Association, the aim of which was to assist Welsh immigrants. He eventually conceived the idea of an independent homeland for the Welsh people who had already settled in America. But, for various reasons, this failed to reach fruition. Jones then thought in terms of Patagonia or a country where a Welsh settlement could be established.

His father was the Principal of Bala College, a theological institution and on his retirement Michael Jones succeeded him in the post.

However, a conflict arose which became dubbed as 'the Battle of the Two Constitutions'. Jones firmly advocated that its subscribers should administer the college while the other camp held that it should be in the hands of representatives appointed by churches throughout Wales. The controversy escalated and the sting in the tail, as it was regarded, was Michael Jones's announcement regarding the Patagonian community:

> There will be chapel, school and Parliament and the old language will be the medium of worship, of trade, of science, of education and of government. A strong and self reliant nation will grow in a Welsh homeland.

He resigned from his post at the college in 1892 in order to devote his time to the establishment of the Bala-Bangor Theological College.

A further important figure who was born in the area was O.M. Edwards (1858-1920). He established himself as a tremendously influential figure in the educational field and was passionate in his belief that the children of Wales should be made aware of the profound importance of the language, culture and history of Wales. He established 'Urdd Gobaith Cymru' in 1922, a movement that aimed to enhance the lives of the youth of the country. It runs two residential centres and organises a well-known annual Eisteddfod. The entry on the organisation, which appears in the *Oxford Companion to the Literature of Wales* claims:

> Its role as a bastion of Welsh national consciousness among the young continues to be of the first importance.

Sheepdogs and Whisky

No account of Bala would be complete without the inclusion of R.J. Lloyd Price, the squire of Rhiwlas Hall, near Fron-goch, a short distance from Bala on the Trawsfynydd road and close to the Tryweryn reservoir.

Price had a number of strings to his bow, but is chiefly remembered today for two reasons. He is the person who can take the credit for introducing sheepdog trials in Britain. In fact, he seems to have been very fond of dogs and even wrote a book entitled, *Tales My Dog Wagged*. But he is also remembered as the man who tried to manufacture and distribute Welsh whiskey and this in an area which professed abstinence.

His company, set up in an attempt to rival the Irish, came into being in 1889 and the promotional hype was, to say the least, colourful.

> Welsh whiskey is the most wonderful whiskey that ever drove the skeleton from the feast or painted landscapes on the brain of man. It is the mingled souls of peat and barley . . .

Price had invested no less than £100,000 in the venture. Because of the puritan outlook of the God-fearing people of Bala it seems that deliveries to local suppliers were made under cover of darkness. A woman depicted on the label of the bottle was, in fact, Price's wife. She was shown riding side saddle on a barrel and the caption read:

Tidings of Priceless Price I bring
Mounted on my Thais
Welsh Whiskey's praises loud I sing
From this lofty dais.
Drink it! Tis brewed on, here's the tip.
The estate of Price of Rhiwlas
Twill Scotch the Irish so a nip
Take each old man and new.

The company eventually ran into severe financial difficulty and when Price's fortunes were at a low ebb he purchased a racehorse named Bendigo. It proved to be a sound purchase for the horse came first in a major race. When he died, Price was buried in the family vault at Llanfor.

He had requested that the following lines be inscribed at his resting place:

As to my latter end I go
To meet my Jubilee,
I bless the good horse Bendigo
Who built this tomb for me.

The University of Revolution

One of the most fascinating historical features of the twentieth century in the Bala area was the direct result of the Easter Rising in Dublin in 1916. P.H. Pearse of the Irish Republican Brotherhood and James Connolly of Sinn Fein led this insurrection, which lasted for six days. To put it in simplistic terms the cause of the rebellion revolved around the issue of home rule and independence from the dictates of the English Government in London.

There was serious street fighting and loss of life and a good deal of this action occurred around or close to the post office in Dublin. It had been hoped that Germany, which was regarded as an ally might lend support but this did not materialise.

Following the surrender of several hundred rebels the authorities began a widespread search for those still at large. This resulted in the total numbers being in excess of four thousand and about half this number were released. This still posed a problem for the authorities, however, for it was agreed that such large numbers of rebels could not be contained in captivity in Ireland, as the mood of the country was dangerously volatile. In the end it was agreed that they should occupy the quarters which, at that time, were occupied by German prisoners of war at Fron-goch. Following the removal of these men the Irish began to arrive. They were among 2,519 prisoners who were deported to various parts of Britain, some of whom were totally unconnected with the Rising. 1,863 found themselves incarcerated at Fron-goch. For some the initial impact was not unpleasant. One of the internees, W.J. Brennan-Whitmore, wrote a memoir of camp life entitled, *With the Irish in Fron-goch*, published in 1917. He observed:

> When we crossed the border our hearts warmed to Wales. It's so like Ireland. We greeted the people in a friendly tone, and invariably received a cheery reply.

But conditions at the camp left a great deal to be desired and Michael Collins wrote to a friend about some of the prisoners having their sleeping quarters close to a steam engine which emitted sickening oil fumes.

The prisoners were responsible for running their own affairs and the authorities failed to anticipate the eventual political result of throwing so many Irish rebels together from widely different backgrounds.

This is highlighted in a paragraph in Whitmore's book:

> What Sandhurst was doing for the British Army, Fron-goch was bidding fair to do for the Irish Republican Army . . . the British Government had swept up the cream of the Irish volunteers and dumped them all down in a huge training camp in North Wales. We had carte blanche in the matter of drilling and military lectures . . . We were certain that by the time we would be released the nucleus of a magnificent military machine would be presented to Ireland.

It is hardly surprising that in Ireland Fron-goch became known as Ollscoil na Reabhbuide – the University of Revolution.

Michael Collins spent much of his time building up contacts with republicans from all parts of Ireland and from

Liverpool. In the words of one writer:

> . . . from this melting pot emerged the revitalised Irish Republican Army. They proceeded to engage the British Government with its vast resources, human industrial and military, in a war of liberation. This led to the withdrawal of the British from twenty six counties of Ireland and this defection was clearly the first major crack in the Empire.

In June 2002 the immense importance of Fron-goch, in both Irish and Welsh history, was commemorated in a joint Irish-Welsh event, which took place at the site where the camp had once stood. The focal point of the event was the unveiling of a plaque perpetuating the memory of a facet in the twentieth century history of Wales which has gone unnoticed by many.

Further Reading:

Sean O. Mahoney: *Fron-goch: University of Revolution*, FRD Terranta, 1987 (out of print)

Desmond Clifford, 'With the Irish in Fron-goch' an article which appeared in *Planet* No.66 (Dec./Jan. 1987-1988)

Lyn Ebenezer: *Fron-goch: and the birth of the IRA*, Gwasg Carreg Gwalch, 2006

Beddgelert

The immense popularity of this charming village is not only due to its wonderful setting, but also the myth concerning the hound Gelert. The story has it that Prince Llywelyn the Great left his hunting dog to guard his baby son while he went out to catch game in the surrounding forest. When he returned he discovered that Gelert's fangs were covered with blood. He was so enraged that he was unable to think straight and immediately assumed that the animal had attacked the child. In a fit of fury he plunged his sword into the side of his faithful four-legged companion. But when he went through to the back of his dwelling he discovered the infant asleep in his cot. The dog had killed a wolf to protect the baby, hence the blood. As a result, his life was lived in a state of remorse.

It would seem that this story derives not from the medieval period but from the eighteenth century. David Pritchard was the first landlord of the Royal Goat Hotel and was anxious to attract visitors to the village. To enable him to fulfil this attempt at early tourist enterprise he enlisted the assistance of two friends and they set about constructing the grave which we see today.

When the Hon. W.R. Spencer visited the area he was very taken by the story of Gelert, which the three village worthies had fabricated and was inspired to write his well-known twenty three verses on the subject. In doing so, he made the village famous beyond the confines of Wales.

Beddgelert stands at the confluence of the Gwynant and the Glaslyn. Within close proximity Aberglaslyn is a delightful location and George Borrow described it as:

> . . . wondrous, rivalling for grandeur and beauty anywhere either in the Alps or Pyrenees.

The Beddgelert area is likely to attract those with a serious interest in Arthurian myth. Dinas Emrys (Fort of Emrys) is a prominent rocky promontory and, according to Geoffrey of Monmouth's *History of the Kings of Britain*, was given to Merlin by Vortigern, the ruler of Britain at some point between

AD 400 and 600. Merlin was a poet, astronomer and all manner of other things and was capable of being metamorphosed into a hawk or other living creature. Eventually, as the result of a vision experienced at the battle of Arfgerydd in around 573, he is thought to have lost his reason. Some have suggested that he could have gone into hiding in Culloden Wood in Scotland where he is said to have spent his days communing with river creatures.

Folk belief has is that he retired to Ynys Enlli (Bardsey Island). Small islands were regarded as versions of paradise or other worlds inhabited by the spirits of the dead. This belief has Arthurian origins for some thought that Arthur was borne to a magic island in the western ocean after being mortally wounded in battle.

At St Mary's Church in Beddgelert an earlier building is incorporated into the structure and it is likely that there could have been a cell on the site in the sixth century.

Within the Celtic tradition there was a strong monastic element. The princes and gentry of the area endowed monasteries, and by the end of the eleventh century the monastery was built of stone. It had become an Augustinian Priory, a resting place for pilgrims on their way to Bardsey Island. The Priory at Beddgelert was one of the oldest in northern Wales, except for the foundation at Bardsey. The north wall of the building is all we see today incorporated as part of St Mary's Church. The Charter of 1286 refers to the Priory as 'The House of the Blessed Mary at Beddgelert'.

The present church was restored in 1880 and has beautiful stained glass windows.

St Mary's Well was to be found near the Royal Goat Hotel. The monks claimed that they could work miraculous cures with its curative waters. There is no trace of it today.

At the end of the eighteenth century there is said to have been a ghost at the Royal Goat Hotel. David Pritchard, the landlord, suddenly died without leaving a will. The ghost wandered about the fields, lanes and village frightening everyone except one old labourer. It confronted the labourer in the stables and had a message for Alice, his wife. He instructed the labourer to tell his wife that she would find golden guineas under the hearthstone, two of which she must give to the labourer. This all came to pass and the restless ghost was never seen again.

On a lighter note, Alfred Bestall made his home in Beddgelert. It was he who, for many years, drew the pictures and created the story lines for the Rupert Bear stories in the *Daily Express*. He was the subject of a full-length biography, which appeared in 2003, several years after his death. The book reveals that he was a particularly genial man.

The highly popular film, 'The Inn of the Sixth Happiness', was made on location in the area in the nineteen fifties. Older people still recall meeting Ingrid Bergman and Robert Donat in the village.

The ashes of the major twentieth century Welsh language poet, T.H. Parry-Williams, are buried in the churchyard. His scholarship and literary achievement resulted in his appointment to the Chair of Welsh at the University of Wales at Aberystwyth in 1920.

Within the last few decades Beddgelert has been affected by the adverse economic circumstances which characterise other parts of Gwynedd.

Tourism is vital to an area such as this, but it has brought with it certain problems, notably traffic congestion and erosion created by the hundreds of walkers who walk in the hills each year.

Betws-y-coed

Betws-y-coed is situated at a point where three rivers converge. The Conwy, which is the largest, emerges from its source at Llyn Conwy, which is close to Ysbyty Ifan. The Llugwy descends from Capel Curig while the Lledr winds its way down from Moel Siabod.

It seems that Hywel y Saer was walking to Conwy during the Elizabethan period. He began his journey in Bala and the Lledr was flooded at the time. He, therefore, used his enterprise and erected a bridge to enable him to complete his journey. The bridge is still in use and is known as Pont-ar-Ledr.

Sarn Elen, the road which the Romans built to link Caerhun with Tomen y Mur near Trawsfynydd crosses the Llugwy at Betws-y-coed.

The celebrated Swallow Falls, a cataract of seething white water, is probably one of the supreme natural phenomena of Snowdonia.

According to folklore, Sir John Wynn of Gwydir (1553-1627) was condemned to spend eternity in the depths of the pool under the Falls until purged of evil. Although described by one historian as 'rumbustious, grasping, litigious' he was, perhaps, not all that different from some other members of the gentry of his period.

A further prominent feature of Betws-y-coed is the Waterloo Bridge. The fine iron structure bears this name because it was constructed in 1815, the year of the Battle of Waterloo.

Betws was on the stage coach route between London and Holyhead. One of the principal inns where visitors sought rest and refreshment was the Royal Oak. A frequent visitor to the inn in the nineteenth century was the Birmingham artist, David Cox. He portrayed many of the best known features of the area, including the Swallow Falls, Pandy Mill and Pont-y-Pair Bridge. He was also asked to paint a sign for the Royal Oak. This is now exhibited in a Birmingham art gallery, along with other works by Cox. When the landlord's daughter died, Cox caught the melancholy atmosphere of the funeral scene in one of his best known works. He himself died in obscurity in 1859 and his contribution to English painting was only later fully appreciated.

Other painters followed in Cox's footsteps and this resulted in something of an artists' colony in the village. This is hardly surprising, for two centuries ago, before the advent of motorised transport and all the stress of modern life, Betws-y-coed must have surely been a place of 'fairy beauty and wild grandeur' to quote George Borrow who was there during his famous walking tour of 1853.

Such was the popularity of the village in Victorian times that the landlord of the Royal Oak built a large hotel in order to accommodate the increasing number of tourists to the area. Many brought their paints, canvases and easels.

The writer and gypsy scholar, Theodore Watts Dunton, set a chapter of his popular novel, *Aylwin*, around the village and Charles Kingsley also knew the area. He would wander in the hills collecting botanical specimens.

During the Edwardian period, Edward Elgar stayed with friends near the village and is reputed to have composed part of 'The Dream of Gerontius' during this period.

On the west bank of the Conwy is St Michael's Church, which has its origins in the fourteenth century. We may safely assume that an earlier holy shrine was situated on the same site as a bowl on the font dates from the thirteenth century. The church is not in use today but anyone with an interest in the history of the area may obtain an insight into the past by reading the inscriptions on the old tombstones which date from the late seventeenth and eighteenth centuries. In the early nineteenth century the village day school was established in the church building.

St Mary's Church, on the other hand, is still very much in use and dates from 1872. Although it does not appear to offer anything of exceptional historic interest, the interior is charming and a welcome haven from the heat of a very warm summer's day.

The Miners Bridge is so named because it was built to enable men employed at the local lead and zinc mines to cross over the Llugwy on their way to work. As in other rural areas of northern Wales, mining for these minerals was an important source of employment. Quarrying also provided work and a woodland walk will take one high above Betws to the melancholy remains of Rhiwddolion, a ruined hamlet where some of the miners had their homes. It is situated eight hundred feet above Betws. Some fruit trees can still be found in the overgrown gardens.

The close-knit community would worship in a very small chapel, which was built in 1869 and this also doubled as a school.

During the Second World War, Dulwich College Prep School was evacuated to Betws and accommodated at the Royal Oak with the classrooms in the stables. In 1942 the boys helped to fight a serious forest fire in the area. The then Head of the Prep School, J.H. Leakey, relates some of the experiences of both teachers and boys in his memoir, *School Errant*.

Within two miles of Betws is Tŷ Hyll ('The Ugly House'), a not very apt description in an age when there is so much architectural ugliness. It now acts as an information centre for the Snowdonia National Park Authority. It dates from a time when any free man could endeavour to obtain freehold rights to common land on the condition that he could build a fireplace and chimney overnight. He would be expected to accomplish this between dusk and dawn the following day, by which time smoke should be issuing from the chimney. If he could do this then he was allowed to complete the building work in his own time.

One of the focal points of interest for visitors to the area is the Conwy Valley Railway Museum, which is situated in the former goods yard of the village station. During the golden age of steam trains it was a hive of activity with farm machinery, foodstuffs in bulk, coal, building material and all manner of other things arriving. The yard was closed in 1964.

Exhibited in the museum are photographs which give one an insight into the rural way of life before the coming of the diesel train. For the benefit of children, a miniature railway does a circuit of the area close to the museum.

Capel Curig

Capel Curig is situated on the A5 between Betws-y-coed and Bethesda in the heart of Snowdonia.

We do not know a great deal about St Curig, from whom the community takes its name, but there are two interesting literary references to him. Giraldus Cambrensis refers to:

> . . . the staff of St Curig, covered on all sides with gold and representing in its upper part the form of a cross.

The fifteenth century bard, Lewis Glyn Cothi, refers to 'the brave knight Curig's coat of mail', which may suggest that at some point he may well have been a soldier.

One of the most interesting historical features of the area is referred to in W. Bezant Lowe's, *The Heart of Northern Wales*, a treasure for anyone with an interest in the past of northwest Wales. He quotes the antiquarian Lysons who tells us that:

> . . . there are considerable remains of a large Roman building on an estate belonging to the Duke of Ancaster, between Capel Curig and Llanrwst, near a place called Bryn Gefeiliau (or the 'Hill of the Smithy') . . . I distinctly traced the walls of two rooms; the dimensions of one were 60 feet by 20 feet and the other was 18 feet 6 inches square, in which where several pillars like those of the Hypocaust under the Feathers Inn in Chester.

The old parish boundaries of Llandygái, Llanllechid, Trefriw, Llanrwst and Dolwyddelan once converged at Capel Curig.

In the nineteenth century Lord Penrhyn was responsible for the building of an inn here, which provided accommodation and refreshment for both coach travellers and pedestrians. The building was enlarged at a later stage and according to one guidebook of the period:

> . . . every curious and contemplative observer of the sublimities of nature will certainly be happy in knowing that the very centre of Eryri has been rendered accessible even by carriage.

A book which put Capel Curig on the map for many readers worldwide was Thomas Firbanks's, *I Bought a Mountain*. In this he describes how he and his wife, Esme, bought and farmed Dyffryn Mymbyr. It proved to be a very tough way of life and is vividly evoked. The landscape is also memorably described, as here:

> The entrance to Dyffryn Valley is guarded by two lakes. The left wall of the valley is the long hump of Moel Siabod and the right wall, higher and more rough, is the Glyders. Across the head of the valley stand Snowdon and her satellites, like maidens hand in hand, barring the way out.

Within close proximity to Capel Curig is one of the most famous hotels in Wales, the Pen-y-Gwryd, which has been much favoured by generations of mountain climbers.

It was in Snowdonia that the successful Everest expedition team of 1953 practised their climbing skills before setting out to attempt the ascent of the highest mountain in the world. They were accommodated at the Pen-y-Gwryd. Chris Briggs, a former owner, who decided to design a special bar to commemorate the achievement, recorded their association with the hotel. Here silver tankards bear the name of members of the expedition and signed photographs of John Hunt, Edmund Hillary, Sherpa Tensing and Charles Evans line the room. The writer Jan Morris was the only journalist to accompany them and her reports appeared in *The Times*.

All these names appear in the visitors' book, along with other luminaries from the climbing world.

There was also a time when some distinguished literary names appeared in the book.

In the Victorian period the poet and novelist, Charles Kingsley, visited the area on an extensive holiday bringing with him two friends, Thomas Hughes, the author of *Tom Brown's Schooldays* and Tom Taylor, an actor and dramatist. Kingsley left some amusing doggerel in the visitors' book:

> Now all I've got to say is
> You can't be better treated
> Order pancakes and you'll find they're the best you've ever eated,

If you scramble o'er the mountains you should bring an ordinance map.

I endorse all 'as previous gents have said about the tap.'

Parts of Kingsley's novel, *Two Years Ago*, are set in the area.

Plas y Brenin Outdoor Activities Centre was established by the Central Council for Physical Recreation and has a considerable reputation for its rock climbing courses.

There is a weather station at Capel Curig and this is the reason why it is quite often mentioned on television weather forecasts in connection with its high levels of rain.

Dinas Mawddwy and Mallwyd

Dinas Mawddwy is situated on the A470 between Dolgellau and Llanbrynmair.

The Lordship of Mawddwy was independent of the remainder of the County of Meirionnydd up to the reign of Henry VIII. Criminality was a major problem in the area and Sir John Wynn determined as a representative of the Crown, to stamp out murder and theft. Many criminals had been taking advantage of the sanctuary provided by the Knights of the Order of St John at Ysbyty Ifan, but were later driven out by Meredudd ap Ifan who was determined that they would no longer be allowed to practise misdeeds in Denbighshire. They fled to the Dinas area and, despite their cunning, Wynn succeeded in capturing eighty of them. They were taken before Judge Lewis Owen, who had a reputation for a lack of restraint when handing down sentences. He sentenced them to death by hanging. The aged mother of one of the accused pleaded with the judge to spare the life of her son, a plea to which he was impervious. The woman then bared her breast and cried out, 'These yellow breasts have given milk to those who wash their hands in your blood'.

The other outlaws were determined to seek revenge on the judge and they hid in a forest through which he frequently passed on his way to Dinas and attacked and slaughtered him without mercy.

When the literary tourist, A.G. Bradley, visited Dinas in the late nineteenth century, he discovered what he interpreted as:

. . . traces in a modified form of the old lawlessness.

Some of the most relentless river poachers in Wales practised their skills here and Bradley observed that even seemingly respectable men of some social status in the community chose not only to turn a blind eye to poaching but, in many cases, to actually encourage it. He writes:

. . . a section of the Welsh bench one might almost suppose

Aberdyfi

Bala

Beddgelert

Betws-y-coed

Capel Curig

Dinas Mawddwy and Mallwyd

Dolgarrog

Dolgellau

Dolwyddelan

Harlech

Llanbedr and Llandanwg

Llanberis

Maentwrog

Penmachno

Talsarnau and Trawsfynydd

Trefriw

Ysbyty Ifan

made it their special and tender care that the idle loafers who net, lime and even dynamite the rivers and lakes of the country shall be shielded from every penalty that the law and the common sense of every civilised country enacts.

In the early nineteenth century the notorious Jack Mytton was High Sheriff of Meirionnydd and he assumed the role of Squire of Dinas Mawddwy. The Mytton family had lived for many generations at Pont-y-Cowryd in the parish of Meifod, although the original family home was at Halston.

Jack Mytton was a larger than life figure who could well have been created by the fertile imagination of the novelist Henry Fielding. He was a gambler and a philanderer whose eccentric lifestyle ensured that his large fortune eventually dwindled to only a few pounds. He rode to hounds and would ride his horse upstairs and over furniture for a wager. He was also in the habit of going out duck shooting in his nightclothes after midnight.

In the nineteenth century the main occupation of the area was either lead mining or, later, the extraction of slate.

When George Borrow visited Dinas in 1853 he was far from impressed by the sight of the 'filthy huts' occupied by the miners in 'a dirty, squalid place'. He goes on:

Fierce looking, red haired men who seemed as if they might be descendants of the red haired banditti of old were staggering about and sounds of drunken revelry echoed from the huts. I subsequently learned that Dinas was the headquarters of miners, the neighbourhood abounding with mines both of lead and stone. I was glad to leave it behind.

On a much more positive note the Rhondda born novelist, Gwyn Thomas, writes of the general area in *The Welsh Eye*:

Drive from the castle of Harlech to Machynlleth and time and again the hillsides seem to stir once more with the hosts of fierce, dark-faced men on their way to join their leader for a last raising of fists against the inclosing trap of English brain and muscle.

Writing of the scenically stunning beauty of the region, A.G. Bradley, described it as:

... delightful, lifted as it is some hundred feet or more above a wooded glen and looking down the valley towards Cemmaes and up to the defiles of Dinas Mawddwy, and across the immense green walls of the Ddolgoed mountains that seem, when mists are rolling in from the sea as they so often are, to touch the very skies.

The effect of the interior restoration work carried out on many Welsh churches in the nineteenth century was generally detrimental, and robbed these buildings of much of their traditional individuality. Mercifully the church at Mallwyd is not among these.

There has been a holy site here since the sixth century when Saint Tydecho established a sanctuary.

A large oak beam, which can be seen above the porch, is dated 1641.

During the mediaeval period, the parishioners, together with those from other parts of Meirionnydd, would graze their cattle on pastureland on the lower slopes of the mountains.

Since 1290 the community has had a succession of priests, but by far the most distinguished is Dr John Davies (c.1567-1644), who contributed greatly to Welsh scholarship during his lifetime.

Born in Denbighshire, he was educated at Jesus College, Oxford, and knew William Morgan when the latter was Bishop of Llandaff.

Davies devoted a great deal of time and energy on the revision of the Welsh Bible and the Book of Common Prayer. He also published a number of other works, including a Welsh grammar. It is worth quoting some words of his, which are recorded in Meic Stephen's invaluable reference work, *The Literary Pilgrim in Wales*:

> It is impossible to believe that God would have seen fit to keep this language until these days, after so many crises in the history of the nation . . . had he not intended His name to be called and his great work to be proclaimed in it.

When George Borrow visited Mallwyd in 1854 he was evidently not particularly interested in either the church or Dr John Davies. Like Kilvert, he always had an eye for feminine beauty and records in some detail a conversation with ' . . . a comely-looking damsel at the bar' of the Brigands Inn. This was so-named because of the activities of the red bandits already referred to.

This small village is situated near the junction of the A470 and the A458.

Dolgarrog

Dolgarrog is situated on the B5106 road between Betws-y-coed and Conwy.

According to a folk tale at some time in the distant past, a dragon named Carrog preyed on livestock in the area and would frequently be seen swooping down over meadowland where it would snare a sheep in its clutches before flying off to its lair again. Local farmers were so outraged that they hunted the creature with spears and pitchforks. But there was one farmer who did not join them. He had been warned in a dream that if he participated in the hunt, Carrog would eventually kill him. A neighbour of his placed the carcass of a sheep near a wood as bait for Carrog and as the dragon alighted on this the men moved forward quickly to attack him. To all intents and purposes he appeared to be dead after what was a forceful assault by the man. However, the dragon performed a final malevolent act when it suddenly and without warning bit the right leg of the farmer already mentioned. He died very soon afterwards.

Fairly close to Dolgarrog are the remains of Maenan Abbey where the Cistercians, the Order of White Monks, practised their faith. We commonly regard the lifestyle of the order as austere and puritanical. It is a little surprising, therefore, to find at least one fifteenth century bard extolling the generosity of the monks in offering him fine meat and wine when he visited them. We read of members of the order unloading casks from a ship moored on the river Conwy. They would then transport these the short distance through meadowland to the abbey.

During the reign of Edward I, the Black Death swept through the lower Conwy Valley and it has been suggested by at least one historian that this may be attributable to a King's officer who, it is thought, may have infected the local population.

A local man is thought to have been connected to some extent with the plot to blow up the English seat of Government, an event that has afforded Guy Fawkes so much prominence.

Thomas Williams (1550-1622) was a cleric and politician and a close friend of Sir John Wynn of Gwydir. It was Wynn who advised Williams not to attend parliament when, as it transpired, Fawkes and his colleagues were arrested. One may wonder how Wynn became privy to this information.

Moving forward to the nineteenth century, a man named John Williams owned a sawmill in the village and exported large quantities of railway sleepers to service an ever-expanding transport network in many parts of Britain.

Industry really came to the village in 1907 when the Aluminium Corporation opened a plant, thus bringing employment to many men of the area.

A power generating station was also established in the first decade of the twentieth century.

Llyn Eigiau and Llyn Cowlyd, both of which had been dammed for the purpose, supplied the water.

On November 2nd, 1925 the wall of the Eigiau dam was breached. Devastating floods followed and a dam was also destroyed near the hamlet of Porth Llwyd. At about nine thirty p.m. some thirty million gallons of water along with large boulders and other debris cascaded down the hillside sweeping away many buildings in its wake. Charles Fred Brown was a boy at the time and on that fateful evening he was enjoying a cinema show in the Assembly Hall, while his parents were at home in Porth Llwyd:

'We were enjoying the film,' he recalled, 'when someone rushed into the hall to tell us that the dam had burst. We rushed outside and ran towards the bridge. I was very concerned about my parents. The rushing water and tumbling boulders made a deafening noise. We heard the church bell ring and someone said that the church had been swept away. We were then taken to a house at the top of the hill and villagers brought along mattresses and blankets. I didn't sleep a wink that night and as dawn broke jumped out of bed to fetch my bike which I had left at the hall where the film show was held, I then cycled miles, calling at farms and houses along the way to enquire about my parents and sisters. Eventually, I was told that my father and my eldest sister had managed to escape but were the only survivors from Porth Llwyd. Sadly, my mother and younger sister were both drowned. You may imagine how I felt. Sixteen adults and children perished. I was totally devastated and the memory of it grieves me to this day.'

The community has now carried out work to commemorate this terrible event.

When a European fund was set up to enable regional projects of various kinds to proceed, money was made available to upgrade certain communities in the Conwy Valley. Dolgarrog wished to create a heritage walk, which would take in the site of the tragedy.

Visitors can now see the mass of boulders, which were carried down by the force of the water, a further reminder of the helplessness of man when confronted by the natural elements when these are out of control.

Dolgellau

Dolgellau can be reached on the A470 from Trawsfynydd, the A494 from Bala, or the A487 north from Machynlleth.

The Romans mined gold in the area and, in fact, coins have been unearthed which bear the name of Emperor Trojan. Gold mining has continued into recent times, until it proved to be no longer commercially viable.

Cymer Abbey, which was situated within close proximity of the town, was built under the patronage of Maredudd ap Cynan in 1199, and was established by the Cistercians.

The Cistercian Order was a disciplined one and its adherents were forbidden to build monasteries within towns. These were therefore erected far from wordly affairs and the main expansion of the Order took place in the north of England and Wales where vast areas of wild and uncultivated countryside gave the monks the opportunity to pursue their pioneering endeavors.

The first monks came from Abbey Cwmhir in Powys and kept sheep in the hills as well as being involved with mining activities. It was never a wealthy institution and following the conflicts of the thirteenth century Cymer's economic position declined still further.

The church has survived, although in a ruinous state and all the evidence suggests that it was a very plain building at a time when so many Cistercian holy sites were beautifully decorated.

Owain Glyndŵr based his parliament in Dolgellau. The building where the proceedings took place can no longer be seen, however. Sir Pryce Jones of Newtown arranged for it to be demolished stone by stone and reconstructed on his estate.

In the reign of Henry IV the estate of Nannau belonged to Howel Gele, a fervent partisan of the House of Lancaster. Owain Glyndŵr was one of his cousins and they did not enjoy a friendly relationship. In an attempt to reconcile these two kinsmen, the Abbot of Cymer arranged a meeting between them at Nannau. All appeared to go well for a time and it was agreed that they should indulge a mutual passion for hunting in a forest on the estate.

Howel had the reputation of being a very skilful archer. As they proceeded they spotted a deer and Howel bent his bow and made pretence of taking aim. This was a devious move, however, for he suddenly turned around to face Owain and released his arrow. But Owain was more than a match for him, being protected by the armour which he wore beneath his clothing. He quickly seized his cousin and later burnt Nannau to the ground.

Nothing was seen of Howel Gele after that, but some fifty years later the skeleton of a man was discovered in the trunk of a large oak tree on the estate. There seemed little doubt that Owain had either succeeded in imprisoning Howel within the tree, where he would have died a horrible death or that he had murdered his attacker and somehow managed to hide the corpse within the oak.

The tree was regarded with considerable superstition in the area for a number of years; indeed some historians have suggested that local people held it in dread.

When Walter Scott read the story of the oak it appealed to him and he included a reference to it in *Marmion*:

All nations have their omens drear,
Their legends wild, of woe and fear.
To Cambria look – the peasant see;
Bethinks him of Glyndowerdy,
And shuns the spirits' blasted tree.

In a final melodramatic twist the tree was later struck by lightning, but Nannau, however, was rebuilt.

In the eighteenth century, Dolgellau was widely regarded as a major town and a nineteenth century writer describes it as being situated in:

. . . a fertile and picturesque vale, bounded by lofty mountains, the sides of which are, in many places, richly clothed with wood and adorned by genteel residences.

During the eighteenth century Dolgellau became prominent as an important centre in the manufacture of woollen cloth. Many of the poor of the area were involved in this trade. It created work for some fifteen hundred employees and the finished products were sent to Liverpool and then found their way to the United States. During the ten years between the end of the America War of Independence and the commencement of the Napoleonic period, the manufacturers established a warehouse at Barmouth and conveyed a third of their products to London. However, the expense involved proved prohibitive and eventually led to a decline in the trade.

The church in Dolgellau dates from 1726 and has a fine thirteenth century effigy of Maurice, son of Ynyr Fychan, an ancestor of the Vaughan's of Nannau. There is also a monument, which perpetuates the memory of Dafydd Ionawr, a nineteenth century bard.

A grammar school for boys was founded in the seventeenth century, one of the earliest grammar schools in Wales, while Dr Williams's well known and highly reputable school for girls came much later. It was opened in 1875.

Elizabeth Baker lived in the area from 1770 until 1778 having come from London in order to administer mining interests. However, it seems that she was outwitted and, as a result, forced to take work as a secretary to Hugh Vaughan of Hengwrt. She kept a record of all her experiences in a diary.

The Quaker leader, George Fox, visited Meirionnydd. It seems that while standing on the slopes of Cader Idris he experienced a vision which convinced him that God ' . . . would raise up a people to himself in this area'. His words won over some converts and the seeds of Quakerism were sown. At Dolgellau, Welshpool and Denbigh there was an encouraging response to the persuasion of Quaker preachers but in areas of north west Wales, which were under the thumb of the gentry the move to a faith which was so unpopular in many circles would not even be considered. The church authorities of the cathedral city of Bangor would not welcome any approach to worship, which did not adhere to their faith. Under a number of different laws, Quakers could be brought to account and punished heavily. It is one of the great paradoxes that religion, which should surely embody love and tolerance, has so long been responsible for intolerance, imprisonment and even torture and murder.

Dolgellau became well known as a hotbed of Quakerism

and, faced with the prospect of persecution or a new life in Pennsylvania, the choice did not prove difficult. Rowland Ellis, a landowner who farmed at Bryn Mawr, bought land in Pennsylvania naming it after his Welsh home. A prestigious women's college later adopted this name.

Within burial grounds in both Dolgellau and Bala, you will discover characteristic squat gravestones where members of the Society of Friends were laid to rest.

The local authorities have established a museum to perpetuate the memory of the Meirionnydd Quakers. This is situated above the tourist information centre in Eldon Square.

The story of the Pennsylvania immigrants has been fictionalised in two novels by Marion Eames, *Y Stafell Ddirgel* (1969) and *Y Rhandir Mwyn* (1972) both of which have appeared in English translations.

While we are in a literary vein, it is worth mentioning that many notable nineteenth century writers visited Dolgellau and the town can boast associations with Walter Scott, Bulmer Lytton, Thomas Love Peacock and George Meredith. But John Torbuck, a legal clerk, records one of the most entertaining impressions of life here in the second decade of the eighteenth century.

His comments on the accommodation, which he was allocated, were scathing although, it has to be admitted, that they make very amusing reading. The bed, for instance, is described and:

> . . . [this] was ascended by a ladder of six or eight steps, so that it was highly necessary for a man to make his will before he went into it, lest, if he had tumbled out in the night he had awakened in another world the next morning . . .

He also complains of 'a regiment of fleas', but that was not all by any means:

> Misfortunes rarely come singly; in the middle of the night in comes a great sow who, I suppose, had been tenant in possession of the room before me, and came to claim re-entry. With this grunting chamber-fellow I was obliged to pass over the night, but never in my whole life before prayed either so heartily or so often.

We do not know which inn Torbuck stayed at and one wonders whether it was the one where William Mackepiece Thackeray stayed when he came to Wales. He left the following lines in the visitors' book:

If ever you come to Dolgelly
Don't stay at the . . . Hotel,
For there's nothing to put in your belly
And no one to answer the bell.

When the immortal diarist, Francis Kilvert, stayed at the Golden Lion in 1871 he was in characteristically romantic mood. He confesses that he was:

. . . very much struck and taken with the waitress . . . She was a beautiful girl with blue eyes, eyes singular lovely, the sweetest, saddest, most wary and most patient eyes I ever saw. It seemed she had a great sorrow in her heart.

John Ruskin certainly loved the beauty and isolation of Meirionnydd and writes that there is only one finer walk than the one from Barmouth to Dolgellau and that is the one from Dolgellau to Barmouth!

I shall end this account of Dolgellau with a brief history of Our Lady of Seven Sorrows.

In 1929 eight Carmelite nuns from London arrived in the town but the church, which they served, was an extremely primitive structure which, prior to their taking it over and converting it, had been a barn and later a fish and chip shop.

The roof was in such a state of disrepair that there were puddles of rainwater on the floor. Because of this the priests who were appointed only stayed for a short time. But Father Eric Green remained for a number of years and achieved a great deal. However, the church, as we see it today, is due to the single-minded vision of Father Francis Scalpell. He was one of three Maltese priests who, having been ordained in Rome, was sent to Liverpool to found the parish of St Anthony of Padua at Moseley Hill. He came to Dolgellau in 1939. Father Scalpell recalled that when he arrived:

As there was no presbytery. I would crawl up a ladder to bed in a barn. Since the roof had lost most of its slates I enjoyed a wonderful view of the stars.

He was not particularly concerned about his own comfort but felt passionately that there should be a suitable place in which mass could be celebrated. This was in time accomplished.

Later, after much hard work, the building was extended. Father Scalpell spoke five languages and so was able to converse freely with Italian prisoners of war who arrived in the area during the 1939-1945 war. Some of these exiles were of great assistance with the practical upkeep of the church.

But, after all his efforts, Father Scalpell still felt that the town deserved 'a proper church'. He, therefore, sent 25,000 letters to various countries requesting donations, and there was an unexpected turn of events. A total stranger stayed behind after mass one day. 'As a matter of interest, how much do you require?' he asked. Father Scalpell named a sum, 'You shall have it,' exclaimed the man.

Shortly afterwards a letter arrived from a solicitor which stated that his client would donate the money on two conditions. The first was that his identity should not be revealed and the second that the building should blend with its environment.

Work on the building took four years to complete and the cost was £68,000.

Father Scalpell died in 1970.

Dolwyddelan

Situated on the A470, south west of Betws-y-coed, Dolwyddelan was once a slate quarrying community.

Within its castle was born one of the immortal heroes of Wales, Llywelyn ap Iorwerth, 'The Great', who obtained the recognition of Welsh rights in Magna Carta following his involvement in the revolt against King John in 1215. He established supremacy over other Welsh Princes. It seems likely that it was Llywelyn who was responsible for the building of the castle, which is located on a rocky ridge above the floor of the Lledr Valley and controlled the area from the Conwy Valley to Meirionnydd.

The castle was a strategic stronghold for Llywelyn ap Gruffudd, who was the grandson of ap Iorwerth, and its capture in 1283 by the English proved to be a turning point in the Edwardian campaign.

It was felt by some that it was taken due to the treachery of one of the inhabitants. The taking of the castle, in the winter, and, at a time when snow lay on the ground, provided an early attempt at military camouflage as Edward I had his army fitted out in white tunics.

Once the castle had been taken and the campaign concluded, the place had little to offer Edward. It was not an easy castle to supply and it was a little distant from the sea. One of the main reasons for Edward's success was his ability to arrange supplies to his garrisons by sea.

In 1488 Meredudd ap Ieuan acquired the site and brought the buildings back into use. He later burnt a house to the south east of the village. The area around Dolwyddelan was troubled by brigands and Meredudd took up the challenge and drove them out. He purchased lands from the Coetmor family of Betws-y-coed and Llanrwst and built the original mansion house at Gwydir at Llanrwst. His eldest son John Wyn ap Meredudd extended the power of Gwydir, thus setting the scene for the rise of the famous Wynn family.

The mediaeval stone coffin of Llywelyn ap Iorwerth can be

found in Gwydir Chapel in the parish of Llanrwst.

Although now much restored, the castle is probably not dissimilar to the castles of the Welsh Princes, as they originally existed.

The founder of the sixteenth century church at Dolwyddelan is thought to have been Gwyddelan. According to Sir John Wynn's *History of the Gwydir Family*, Meredudd ap Ieuan

> . . . after he had lived certaine yeares at Dolwyddelan castle builded the house in Penamnen, being the principal best ground in Dolwyddelan, and alsoe within certaine yeares after, he removed the church of Dolwyddelan from a place called Brin y bedd, to the place where now it is, being part of the possessions of the priory of Bethgelert. He also there new-built the same as it is now, one crosse chapell excepted, which my uncle Robert Wynn built.

There is a stained glass window in the church. It is known that Meredudd had visited Rome twice and it could be that having seen the wide Renaissance church windows in Italy he decided that one of a similar kind would be appropriate at Dolwyddelan.

Certain alterations were authorised by Lord Willoughby de Eresby shortly before 1850.

Harlech

The historian, Lewis Lloyd, who spent much of his time researching the past of Ardudwy, confessed to a distinct feeling of unease whenever he visited Harlech Castle:

> 'I feel like an intruder,' he wrote, 'and is it mere fancy on my part to detect an air of bold assurance in the bearing of many English visitors as they enter the castle and walk around its battlements?'

In Harlech, as in so many other parts of Wales, the atmosphere of the past is almost palpable. Situated between a rugged and bleak hinterland and a magnificent coastal plain this grey-stoned community seems almost to have evolved from the rock, which is such a prominent geological feature of the area.

The castle is one of the fortifications which Edward I built in his attempt to subjugate northern Wales and work on it was completed somewhere around 1283. The most impressive feature is probably the gatehouse where the constable of the castle had his apartments.

It is concentric in shape and there are four projecting round towers. James of St George was responsible for the design and overall supervision of the building. He was rewarded by being appointed constable by Edward. There is evidence to suggest that a very large number of men were employed on the building work, 940 in total according to Dr Lloyd. These included the smiths, carpenters and masons as well as the men who quarried the stone in the surrounding hills.

Writing in the seventeenth century the historian, Saxton, wrote of an event, which occurred in 1467:

> Hard by the sea in the little territory named Ardudwy the Castle Harlech, in times past named Caer Colun, standeth advanced upon a very steep rock and looketh down into the sea from aloft, which being built as the inhabitants report by King Edward the First, took name of the situation. For Arlech in the British tongue signifieth as much, as upon a

stony rock. While England was disjointed with civil broiles, David ap Ienkin ap Einion a noble Gentleman of Wales, who took part with the House of Lancaster, defended it stoutly against King Edward the Fourth; until that Sir William Herbert, Earl of Pembroke, making his way with much adoe through the midst of these mountains of Wales, no leesse passable than the Alpes, assaulted the castle in such furious thundering manner that it yeelded into his hands. Incredible it is almost what a cumbersome journye hee had of it, and with what difficulty hee got through, while he was constrained in some places to climbe up the hilles; in others to come down tumbling, both he and his company together. Whereupon the dwellers thereabout call that way to this day Le Herbert.

It was David (or Dafydd) who, according to a traditional story, boasted that he once held a castle in France for such a long period that even the old women of Wales had heard of his feat. He was reputed to have proclaimed that he would hold Harlech Castle until every old woman in France knew of it.

Following the defeat of Henry VI at Northampton in 1640, Margaret of Anjou, his wife, sought refuge in the castle for a time.

When Owain Glyndŵr spearheaded his campaign for an independent Wales he launched a successful assault on the castle. The Yorkists were defeated and taken into captivity. They had hoped that troops would come from Conwy but these failed to arrive. It is thought by some that the world famous song, 'Men of Harlech', was composed as a result of this conflict.

Although parts of the castle were in ruins by the time of the Civil War, Harlech was held for the King and only surrendered to Parliamentary forces in 1647, the last Royalist outpost to do so.

It is possible that there may well have been an earlier and probably much more modest fortification situated on the gigantic area of rock on which Harlech Castle was built. The fort was named Tŵr Branwen (Tower of Branwen), a title which linked it to one of the most mysterious tales in the *Mabinogion*.

It is on this rock that the story opens. Matholwch, the King of Ireland, arrived to claim the hand of the ill-fated Branwen in marriage. Their subsequent married life was intended as a symbolic gesture to unite Britain and Ireland.

For the first year of the marriage they were happy but their union was disrupted when old grievances between the two countries were rekindled and Matholwch's brother's attempt to settle old scores. As a result, Branwen was humiliated by being forced to work as a kitchen maid. She reared a starling and taught it to say her name. She later ordered it to fly to Wales to find her brother, Bendigeidfran. When he learned of the circumstances in which his sister was now living he was enraged and set off across the Irish Sea. In the resulting battle much blood was spilled and there were only seven survivors. Branwen returned to Wales where she died of grief.

This story has provided creative stimulus for a number of writers and visual artists and within close proximity to the castle you will find a work of bronze sculpture by Ivor Roberts-Jones entitled, 'Y Ddau Frenin' (The Two Kings). It depicts Bendigeidfran returning from Ireland bearing the body of Branwen's son, Gwern. It effectively symbolises the universal futility of war.

Harlech assumed the status of principal town in the region by the mid-sixteenth century and the Quarter Sessions were established there. Corruption was rampant among the privileged classes then. Many were prepared to employ any means at their disposal in order to obtain additional land; money, status and bribery were commonplace. It is not so surprising, therefore, that so much of the financial and legal documentation from the period has not survived.

Later the Quarter Sessions moved to Dolgellau and, as a result, Harlech lost much of its status.

The legal wrangling between the families of the gentry continued through the eighteenth century but at least they now sought legal resolutions as opposed to taking the law into their own hands.

The ordinary people – the term working class had not come into usage then – eked out a living on the partly drained marshlands and the many acres of rocky ground in the hills.

When William Bingley visited Harlech in 1798 he observed:

Once the principal town of Merionethshire, it is now dwindled into an insignificant village, containing not more than four or five hundred inhabitants.

When he came in 1808, Richard Fenton described it in even more negative terms:

It is a rather poor village . . . the most forlorn, beggardly place imaginable . . . The building they show you for the Town Hall is ruinous and unroofed . . .

Landowners drained the low lying land or the Morfa, as it is known, and the now familiar pattern of fields replaced a wilderness of marsh. This created a problem, however, for it meant that the townspeople who previously had grazing rights on this land now had to look elsewhere.

In 1835 Harlech lost its borough status.

In the second half of the nineteenth century the men folk of the town were involved in maritime activity, slate quarrying, lead mining and, of course, farming.

This period saw the arrival in the area of steam trains and Victorian Harlech became the home of a number of upper class English families. Some resided in their Welsh homes through the year while others spent only their summers there.

'Members of a new ascendancy, which was superimposed upon the local and native middle class, dispensed patronage in various forms,' writes Lewis Lloyd.

There was an annual music festival of a high standard, which, before the advent of radio ensured that the people of Meirionnydd had access to the works of the great composers. The distinguished list of luminaries who performed at the festival included Sir Adrian Boult, Sir Malcolm Sergeant and Walford Davies.

A library and institute was established and a golf course, which is regarded as one of the finest in Wales, was created.

Among those who settled in the town was A.P. Graves and his family. One of his sons was the poet, Robert Graves, and in his celebrated autobiography, *Goodbye to All That*, he recalls his childhood period in the area. In the nineteen fifties his sister, Clarrisa, was a familiar, if eccentric, local figure.

The Plas Café on the High Street is a very elegant building with a fine conservatory. In 1905 it became the home of a family named Finch-Hatton. Dennys Finch-Hatton was immortalised in Karen Blixen's book, *Out of Africa*. Robert Redford portrayed him in the very popular screen version of the book.

A particularly interesting figure in the twentieth century history of the town is George Davison. He was the European director of Eastman-Kodak and was, politically, extremely left wing.

He purchased Plas Wernfawr, a large house in the town. He was very generous to children from poor families and would invite them to his home for cakes and lemonade. This was at a time when socialist summer schools were held at nearby Llanbedr and when Bernard Shaw visited one of these he took time off to visit his friend Davison at Harlech. Incidentally, Shaw decided to take a lone walk in the Rhinog hills and managed to get himself lost in low cloud. This resulted in his arriving back at Llanbedr a couple of hours late.

The period of economic depression following the First World War inevitably brought unemployment to Harlech, as it did to communities throughout Wales. It was, therefore, very much a place of human contrasts. On the one hand, were the poor working class, desperately hoping for work, while the affluent spent their days in comfort and luxury.

In 1927, Wernfawr ceased to be a private house and was transformed into an independent residential college for adults. The Civil Servant, Thomas Jones, who played such an important role in Welsh political life, was the guiding spirit behind the establishment of Coleg Harlech, where I was once a student. Jones was fully committed to the belief that the working class should be allowed a second chance as far as education was concerned and, in fact, Coleg Harlech is frequently referred to as 'the college of the second chance'. Over the years, it has had a distinguished staff, including Ben Bowen-Thomas, who was the first warden; T. Rowland Hughes, D. Tecwyn Lloyd, Gwyn Erfyl Jones, Dafydd Ellis Thomas and Richard Poole. Most of these have, in different ways, made their mark in the field of Welsh literature, while writers can also be numbered among past students including the poet, Bryn Griffiths, and the novelist, Ron Berry.

But we must not overlook an earlier writer who is closely associated with Harlech. Ellis Wynn (1671-1734) was born at Y Lasynys, a farmhouse situated just outside the town. He was the author of *Gweledigaethau'r Bardd Cwsg* (Visions of the Sleeping Bard). He was educated at Jesus College, Oxford, and ordained an Anglican priest in 1704. He became the Rector of Llanbedr and Llandanwg and died in 1774. He is buried under the altar of the church in Harlech.

Further Reading:
Lewis Lloyd: *The Book of Harlech*, Barracuda Books, 1991
O. Wynn Hughes: *Every Day was Summer: Childhood Memories of Edwardian Days in a Small Welsh Town*, Gomer, 1989
Peter Stead: *Coleg Harlech: The First Fifty Years*, University of Wales Press, 1977

Llanbedr and Llandanwg

Llanbedr is situated some three miles from Harlech on the A496 Harlech – Barmouth road.

The Church of St Pedr has an englyn carved over the door, this being the oldest known metrical form of Welsh poetry. There are free standing Neolithic carved stones near the font, which are of archaeological significance. On the south wall are two beautiful pre-Raphaelite stained glass windows, which perpetuate the memory of a family named Pope.

Lewis's *Topographic Dictionary* (1863) has this to relate about the church:

> The church dedicated to St Peter is an ancient structure; according to an absurd local tradition it was originally intended to erect it at a place within forty yards to the right of the road, where are four or five broad stones, eight feet high, standing upright; but the workmen found what they executed by day was removed at night, and therefore commenced the building on its present site.

At the time that Lewis was writing, the provisions of an Act of Parliament relating to the reclamation of the waste land of Llanbedr and the neighbouring parishes had been passed. Nine hundred and forty acres were enclosed at Llanbedr.

The Artro river runs through the village from its source in the Rhinog hills at Cwm Bychan.

Legend has it that a weir once stood at the mouth of the river and that this was granted by Gwyddro Goronhir to his son, Elphin. One day, Elphin discovered a babe in arms in a coracle and this child turned out to be none other than the bard Taliesin.

There is a farmhouse in nearby Cwm Nantcol, which is built on the site of a previous residence. This was the home of the Lloyd family who settled here during the mediaeval period. Their ownership of the property came to an end in the nineteenth century. When he was travelling around northern Wales in the late eighteenth century, Thomas Pennant visited the member of the Lloyd clan resident there at the time:

> I was introduced to the worthy representative of this long
> line, who gave me a most hospitable reception, and in the
> style of any Ancient Briton. He welcomed us with ale and
> potent beer, to wash down the Coch y Wden, or hung goat,
> and the cheese compounded of the milk of cow and sheep .
> . . The family lay in their whole store of winter provisions,
> being inaccessible a great part of the season by reason of
> snow. Here they have lived for many generations, without
> bettering or lessening their income, without noisy fame but
> without any embittering attendants.

One of the Lloyd family, Dafydd Lloyd, achieved honour
when he followed the banner of Henry Tudor in his progress
across Wales to Bosworth in 1485. In this notable battle he is
reported to have fought with both skill and tenacity and, as a
result, was commemorated in a song called, 'Farewell Dai
Lloyd', which was popular in Wales in the nineteenth century.

Another farm which is situated in the Rhinogs is Maes y
Garnedd. This was the home of John Jones (1597-1660). He
married twice and his second wife was the sister of Oliver
Cromwell.

Jones was a fervent Parliamentarian and religious zealot
and, to quote the words of Professor Geraint H. Jenkins, 'he saw
the civil war as a means of advancing God's cause by force of
arms'. He became a Colonel in Cromwell's army and was
involved in some of the major sieges of the conflict. His was one
of the signatures on the death warrant of Charles I. But
following the Restoration he was himself arrested and executed.

In *Highways and Byways of North Wales*, A.G. Bradley
writes that:

> . . . Cwm Bychan was a much more frequented place in the
> days of the Romans than in the days of the Lloyds.

Possibly he was thinking of the so-called Roman Steps, a
series of unknown slabs of rock of unknown origin of which
there are some two thousands. This is dubious, however, for
some historians have claimed that there is no concrete evidence
to suggest that the Romans occupied the area. A more widely

held belief is that they were created in mediaeval times.

Llyn Cwm Bychan is a beautiful lake 505 feet above sea level.

Despite the low flying aircraft, which carry out training exercises in the sky above, one can still experience a sense of considerable isolation in these hills and for most of the time the only sounds to be heard are the lonely call of the curlew and the larks.

In earlier times one might well have heard the sound of a hunting horn breaking the silence. Bradley refers to the strict regulations, governing hunting, which were legally imposed in both Cwm Bychan and Cwm Nantcol.

'No one,' he writes, 'was allowed to carry a horn till he had passed an examination in the laws of the chase'.

He goes on to tell us 'no hoofs but those of the nimble mountain sheep tread the patchy turf that grows between the grim and naked rocks'.

This may have been true then but is no longer the case. Nowadays the walker will spot, without too much difficulty, the wild white goats which roam these hills, as well as the wild ponies.

Manganese, a grey brittle metallic element, was mined here and abandoned mine shafts can also be seen at various points.

It was at Cwm Nantcol that the painter, Curnow Vosper (1866-1942), produced a work, which has become a Welsh icon. This was the very well known 'Salem', so named because it was painted within the small Baptist chapel of that name, situated approximately a mile and a half from Llanbedr. It depicts a rather miserable looking old woman in traditional nineteenth century Welsh dress. She is wearing a rather fine looking shawl and in the folds of this, if one looks carefully, one may see the face of the devil. The woman's name was Siân Owen and, according to one source, she was very vain. Those of a Freudian turn of mind may choose to think that the presence of the devil in the painting is due to this sense of vanity. But, on the other hand, Vosper once said that the shawl had been borrowed for the occasion from the wife of the then Vicar of Harlech. So one can draw one's own conclusions about that! For a time the work was exhibited in the Royal Academy and later became an advertisement for a brand of soap manufactured by Lever

Brothers at Port Sunlight.

Siân Owen lived on until 1933 but it seems that her life was dogged by misfortune.

Moving down to Llandanwg, Mochras, or Shell Island as it is more popularly known, is within very easy walking distance. It is a peninsula so named because of the large number of shells to be found there.

The church is situated close to the sea and sand frequently covers part of the churchyard.

It was originally the parish church of Harlech and the font was removed there many years ago.

Siôn Phylip, one of a family of bards in Ardudwy, and born in 1543 is buried here. He eked out a living as a farmer and supplemented his meagre income through writing.

He is one of the last of the itinerant poets of his period and found favour with the Wynn's of Gwydir who became his patrons.

Llanberis

Llanberis is situated on the A4086 between Capel Curig and Caernarfon.

There are two lakes in the area. Nant Peris was initially the focal point around which the local population settled. But as time went on the village of Llanberis grew in size and to some extent Nant Peris began to be of lesser importance as a community.

The names Peris and Padarn have their origin in a period when the Christian faith was followed in what today might be considered a rather elementary way. Understandably, our knowledge of the early saints is very limited and folklore has sometimes tended to obscure truth. But it seems that Saint Padarn established his cell on a site close to that now occupied by the Victoria Hotel.

If you visit Nant Peris you will discover an ancient well associated with him. The nearby church is also worth a visit and contains a beautiful chancel screen from the Elizabethan period.

In Llanberis is situated the larger church of Sant Padarn, a building which dates from the mid-nineteenth century.

Dolbadarn Castle was one of the Welsh fortresses built in order to defend the area from invading English warriors.

It is thought to have been built in the first decade of the thirteenth century and occupies a rocky platform close to Llyn Padarn. The early history of the castle is fairly obscure due to the lack of documentation for that period but there appears to be some evidence to suggest that it could well have replaced Caernarfon as an administrative military centre.

The kingdom of Gwynedd became unsettled and divisive following the death of Llywelyn and his son. But a rather uneasy concord followed when Llywelyn ap Gruffudd, the Prince of Wales, defeated his rivals in 1255. His elder brother, Owen Goch, was among these and Llywelyn sought revenge by imprisoning him in a dungeon at the castle for twenty years. But eventually Llywelyn provoked the wrath of Edward I and within twelve years the Welsh nation found itself under the subjugation of the English.

In 1282 when the English king was conducting his second bout of warfare against the Welsh, Dolbadarn fell to the Earl of Pembroke and not very long after this the structure of the building began to decay.

Owain Glyndŵr is said to have incarcerated his arch enemy, Lord Grey of Rhuthun, at Dolbadarn but some historians have their doubts about this, regarding it, perhaps, as yet a further attractive piece of anecdotal folklore.

The quarrying of slate has been a major industry in northern Wales for many centuries. During the Roman occupation slate was used in the building of Segontium at Caernarfon.

In the early nineteenth century the transportation of slate in the Llanberis area was dependent on the use of boats. Vast quantities would be taken across the lake to Penllyn, Cwm-y-Glo and then on to Caernarfon by horse and cart. But a far more effective method of transportation began when slate was sent by rail from Llanberis to the port at Felinheli on the Menai Straits. From there ships would take the substantial quantities on board to countries across the world.

At one time, three thousand men laboured in extremely unpleasant conditions in order to extract the slate. Their working environment was not only unpleasant but also extremely dangerous. Between 1822 and 1876 there were no fewer than two hundred and twenty fatal accidents at the Dinorwic Quarry, the most common causes of death being injury from falling stones, falls from high places and injuries inflicted during blasting operations.

But despite all of this, the quarrymen were optimistic and intelligent individuals.

During their leisure hours they would discuss the political issues of the day in the wooden cabins in which so many of them lived throughout the week. Many of them were cultured men, some of whom read and even wrote poetry. It is not surprising, therefore, that when a subscription fund was set up in connection with the proposal to establish a university at Bangor, it was the pennies collected by the northern Wales quarrymen, which were the first to be donated.

In 1860 a quarryman's hospital was built on the slopes above Llyn Padarn. In 1892, Dr R.H. Mills Roberts arrived to take charge of it.

Following his arrival football was introduced in the village before it became commonplace in other parts of Wales. Roberts had considerable professional experience of the game, having been goalkeeper for a major English team. He had also played for Wales seven times and so became an asset to Llanberis not only due to his medical skills but also his sporting prowess. He was the guiding spirit behind the village team and was soon nicknamed, 'Dr Goalie'. Games were organised as fundraising events.

During Roberts's period the men organised a 'shilling club'. Under this scheme a shilling was deducted from the wages of each man every week and in the event of an accident he would be eligible for medical care without any further cost. But the men were expected to pay for medicine and other requirements. This has been described as the first occupational health scheme in Britain and it only came to an end with the foundation of the National Health Service in 1948.

Apart from being compassionate, inspired in his medical achievements and supremely energetic, Mills Roberts was a considerable innovator.

He designed metal skull plates and artificial limbs. One of his patients was Edward Jones who lost both arms in a blasting accident. Roberts devised two metal arms to enable him to at least use a knife and fork. Although the hospital was intended primarily for the quarrymen, women and children were eventually treated there as well.

The hospital is now a museum where visitors can see photographs on display as well as some of the instruments used by Mills Roberts.

Of all the communities within the National Park region, Llanberis probably attracts more guaranteed visitors than any other location. After all, it is from the village that one commences the ascent of 3,943 feet by rail to the summit of Snowdon. Although the railway was not opened until 1896, the idea had been conceived over two centuries previously.

The actual construction of the line to the summit was physically daunting, as it meant that the men involved had to labour in very rugged terrain at high altitudes in all kinds of weather conditions both winter and summer. The line has not been entirely accident free.

In 1952 an RAF Anzon aircraft ran into a very severe belt of weather while flying over Snowdon en route from Northern Ireland. It crashed into the mountain and part of the burning wreckage fell on to the railway line at a point, which had just been passed by a train on its return journey to Llanberis from the summit.

Copper mining was another important part of the local economy and one can still see shafts in the hills from which the mineral was extracted, together with the occasional rusted item of machinery and the ruins of buildings where part of the work was carried out. Some fifty men are known to have been employed in the oldest mine, which was situated above Nant Peris. The famous Miners Track, which takes the energetic walker to the summit of Yr Wyddfa, will take you close to the workers' barracks at Llyn Teyrn and on to a further focal point of the industry at Glaslyn.

By its very nature, the work proved exacting and dangerous. It was only possible to work on some of the higher sites in the summer months because access was hazardous in winter weather.

It was not only men who worked in the mines, for the task of breaking the ore often fell to women and children. After it had been broken up it would be taken to Caernarfon by horse and cart and from there loaded on to a trading vessel which would take it on the second stage of the journey to Swansea.

In the eighteenth century a phenomenal woman named Margiad uch Ifan lived in the Nant Peris area. She was well known for her physical strength and it was she who brought the copper ore across Llyn Peris by boat. She is even reputed to have built her own boats. She would go out on hunting expeditions with the best huntsmen and could shoe horses as well as any blacksmith. It may come as a surprise, therefore, to discover that such a masculine woman had many male admirers. But, according to Thomas Pennant, she favoured the most effeminate of these. She died in 1789 at the age of 102.

The Dinorwic Power Station, opened in 1984, is a massive pump storage scheme. The underground cavern was created by excavating three million tons of rock. It was then possible to accommodate a building of sixteen storeys, which is a hundred and eighty meters long and twenty-four meters wide. When it was opened it was described by one newspaper as 'the biggest civil engineering contract ever awarded in British industrial history'. It is now among the top tourist attractions of northern Wales and the complex also includes a café and a centre where one can learn something about the site through the medium of film and interactive displays.

Llanberis also has a lake railway. The line, which is narrow gauge, travels around Llyn Padarn.

Maentwrog

The A497 road from Porthmadog to the Maentwrog valley offers some of the most strikingly beautiful scenery in the whole of Wales. In the eighteenth century the valley was a tidal marsh with little land, which was suitable for cultivation. On a visit here at that time Lord Lyttleton observed:

> With the woman one loves, with the friend of one's heart, and a good study of books one might pass an age in this vale and think it a day. If you have a mind to live long and renew your youth, come and settle in the Ffestiniog valley. Not long ago there died in that neighbourhood an honest Welsh farmer, who was 106 years of age.

It comes as no surprise to learn that the area figures in the pages of the Mabinogi, that unique collection of very early Welsh tales, which still appears on Welsh bestseller lists.

The area is associated with one of the four principal tales of the *Mabinogion*. The two protagonists were Math and Pryderi. Math was the Lord of Gwynedd while Pryderi was the ruler of a region of South Wales.

Gwydion, who lived in Gwynedd, stole Pryderi's pigs. When the two men met, there was some unpleasantness, but eventually they were able to treat each other with respect. But Pryderi was tricked by Gwydion for, at a point on the river Dwyryd approximately a mile from Maentwrog they fell into mortal combat:

> And by dint of strength and valour and by magic and enchantment Gwydion conquered and Pryderi was slain. And at Maen Tyriawg, above Y Felenrhyd, was he buried, and his grave is there.

Our knowledge of the area during the Roman and Dark Ages is very limited but in the fourteenth century a clearer picture emerges. We know, for example, that the land on which Plas Tan-y-bwlch stands was then situated within the township of Ffestiniog, which later became a parish.

In his invaluable short history of Tan-y-bwlch, *The House on a Hill*, Gwyndaf Hughes informs us that the estate was founded by Ieuan ap Iorwerth ap Adda, who died in 1530. He was a descendant of Gruffudd ap Cynan, Prince of Gwynedd, in the late eleventh and early twelfth centuries.

In the sixteenth century the owner was Ieuan ap Robert Evans, whose grandson, Evan Evans, became High Sheriff of Meirionnydd in 1635 and his son, Robert, married Lowri Prys.

We now move forward to the eighteenth century when the Oakeley family took charge of the estate.

In 1789 William Oakeley married Margaret Gruffydd, the heiress of Tan-y-bwlch. Oakeley was responsible for the drainage work in the valley and the erection of embankments to encompass the tidal river within its banks. He also rebuilt the church and was largely responsible for the building of the road from the point where the Oakeley Arms now stands to Llanfrothen and Aberglaslyn. This replaced a rough track, which took travellers via Croesor.

The estate was inherited by William Gruffydd Oakeley and he spent substantial sums on it. He erected a number of buildings including what is now the Old Rectory Hotel. He also had a quarry and the limestone from this was used in building work.

In 1823 he moved to Berkshire and leased the land to Samuel Holland, a Liverpool businessman. This resulted in Oakeley receiving royalties for every ton of slate from a small area of the estate where it was being quarried. What began, to quote one source, as 'a hole with three men working in it' was transformed into a quarry employing no fewer than 1,600 men. At that time it was reputed to be the largest site of its kind. Holland had a son, also named Samuel, who was destined to play an important role in the history of slate quarrying in northern Wales.

The initiative of the Hollands greatly benefited the Oakeley family financially. Although not involved with the industry at first hand, they guarded their interests zealously and in 1929 W.G. Oakeley sued none other than Baron Rothschild. An agent acting on the Baron's behalf had trespassed on the Tan-y-bwlch estate while assessing it as a potential area for mineral extraction. There followed a legal wrangle which the Oakeleys won.

They also played a significant role in the often complex early history of the Ffestiniog railway. Up to then, the extracted slate had been conveyed from the quarries by horse and cart to the trading vessels at Porthmadog. Oakeley realised that if a faster means of transportation could be used then this would increase his royalties considerably. Before the railway line could be constructed, however, an Act of Parliament had to be passed. There were a number of objections to the project from landowners who protested against the loss of their agricultural land. But despite everything, W.G. Oakeley achieved his aim and he himself laid the foundation stone in February 1833.

Two years later Oakeley died and the estate was inherited by Louisa Jane, a cousin's widow, Oakeley having died childless. She had a shrewd business brain and the royalties brought her wealth. She provided the money for the building of a hospital for quarry workers in Blaenau Ffestiniog.

But, as time went on, she became obstinate by nature and began to lose interest in the management of the estate. In 1868 she left Tan-y-bwlch with a servant and took with her the family silver. She stayed at a hotel in Shrewsbury. A further member of the family, William Edward, became convinced that Louisa had lost her reason and consulted a doctor about this. The doctor, however, dismissed the idea. When she died in London in 1878 William Edward inherited Tan-y-bwlch and the estate.

He carried out a number of improvements and formed what became known as the Oakeley Slate Quarry Company, borrowing large sums in order to make this possible. In 1883 a slump occurred but, as his business interests and his lavish lifestyle demanded a large and steady income, he reached a point where he was forced to mortgage the estate. Trustees were appointed to take over the leasing arrangements of the quarries. But when pressure was exerted regarding the repayments of loans serious difficulties arose and in 1902 much of the land was sold. In 1910, the remainder was auctioned at Chester.

Tan-y-bwlch is now the Study Centre for the Snowdonia National Park and courses on many interesting subjects are held there throughout the year. Many of these are related, in one way or another, to the heritage of this wonderful part of the world.

The village obtained its name from the very large stone to be found in the churchyard. It seems likely that it originally stood beside a Roman road leading to nearby Tomen y Mur. However, it is also an integral part of local legend. Twrog was a giant at some very distant period of the past and, it seems that he hurled the stone from the summit of a hill, aiming it presumably at whatever place of worship may have existed there at the time. It might have been a pagan site, which would explain Twrog's action, for he was, it seems, a very devout Christian. Interestingly the stone, for whatever reason, is different in a geographical sense from other rocks which have been examined in the area.

It has been argued that Twrog was a saint of the early Celtic church, living in the sixth or seventh century.

St Twrog's Church has a west window which commemorates Edmwnd Prys who was Rector of Maentwrog and Ffestiniog from 1572 to 1626. A notable poet and scholar he metrically translated the psalms into Welsh. A native of Llanrwst, he combined his clerical life with the lifestyle of a country gentleman.

The entry on him, which appears in *The Oxford Companion to the Literature of Wales*, states:

> Edmwnd Prys was a unique figure among Welsh poets of his period, being steeped in both the humanistic learning of the Renaissance and the traditional culture of his native land.

The novelist and poet, Thomas Love Peacock, spent the period from 1810-1811 in Maentwrog and it is claimed that when he came to write his novel, *Headlong Hall*, the mansion he depicted was based on Plas Tan-y-bwlch. He married Jane Griffith, a relative of a family of that name who lived at Plas Tan-y-bwlch at the time.

The area also has a link with a later literary figure, the major nineteenth century English poet, Gerard Manley Hopkins. It seems that as a young man he took a holiday in Wales and was much attracted by all he saw around him. He visited a waterfall close to Maentwrog and, as a result, wrote this short poem:

At a Welsh waterfall

It was a hard thing to undo this knot.
The rainbow shines, but only in the thought
Of him that looks. Yet not in that alone.
For who makes rainbows by invention?
And many standing round a waterfall
See one bow each, yet not the same to all,
But each a hand's breadth further than the next.
The sun on falling waters writes the text
Which yet is in the eye or in the thought.
It was a hard thing to undo this knot.

Penmachno

Penmachno is situated three miles from Betws-y-coed on the B4406.

It derives its name from its position close to the source of the Afon Machno, which rises in the south west and joins the Conwy. In the eighteenth century the village was in the union of Llanrwst and, at one point, the inhabitants numbered 1,274.

Penmachno's main claim to fame lies in its association with Bishop William Morgan (1545-1604), the translator of the Bible into the Welsh language. He was born in a cottage called Tŷ Mawr (Large House) in the valley called Wybrnant.

In his brief biography of Morgan, Richard Tudor Edwards paints a vivid picture of what Wybrnant would have been like in those distant days:

> 'To visit Tŷ Mawr and Wybrnant today is an experience which is akin to going backwards in time. To have visited it in that year in the sixteenth century must, for the townsman have been like going back to the beginning of time. In that century, when the present narrow and pitted roads to Wybrnant must have been little better than paths through the forest and undergrowth, regular visits to Wybrnant would have been enough to daunt anyone but the hardiest Welshman'.

Morgan was the second son of John ap Morgan ap Llywelyn and his wife, Lowri, who were Catholics. It was the custom of the squire of Gwydir to make provision for the education of the children of tenants on the estate. Sir John Wynn's chaplain, therefore, supervised Morgan's education. He displayed considerable ability and went on to Cambridge to continue his education. Here he studied Latin, Greek and Hebrew, the original languages of the Bible. He eventually became a Doctor of Divinity and was the Vicar of Llanrhaeadr-ym-Mochnant from 1578 to 1595. During this period he was engaged in the translation of the Bible into Welsh. This was a remarkable achievement when one takes into account the fact that he worked far from any centres of learning and was not in touch with the intellectual developments of the world beyond.

Through his translation he is regarded as being responsible for the preservation of the Welsh language. Although he was not the only person involved in translation works on the Bible his achievement was outstanding.

He was buried in the Cathedral of St Asaph, beneath the stone in the presbytery and there is a memorial to him and other translators on the north side.

Tŷ Mawr is situated some distance to the north west of Penmachno and is now a National Trust property.

A further important religious figure who came from Penmachno was Roderic Llwyd. As a boy he was reputed to have a mischievous nature and was a practical joker. His parents entertained high expectations as to his future and wished him to become a bishop. They were evidently fairly affluent for they were able to educate him in London. He then went on to Oxford to complete his studies and it is possible that during this period he may well have become acquainted with the poet, John Milton. He held radical ideas concerning the role of the priesthood which may have made him unpopular in certain quarters.

But he began to take a keen interest in legal matters and eventually became a member of the court of Charles I.

St Michael's Church was built on a site which, according to Bezant Lowe, was originally the location where two previous churches may have once stood. Traces of one of these have been unearthed in the churchyard and it is thought that the second could well date to the thirteenth century.

There was a time when it was customary to ring the church bell at nine o'clock in order to summon worshippers for services at ten o'clock. It seems that a local cleric was peeved by the indolence of some of the parishioners which resulted in their missing the service. He, therefore, arranged for the bell to be rung earlier so that they would have no excuse for absence.

The Old School was built in 1840 and in 1905 was converted into a dwelling house. It was occupied by the Sexton for a time and later became a church room for children's meetings.

A contemporary account from the nineteenth century stated that the district 'abounds with mineral wealth; the soil of the valleys is fertile and the fields are productive and in a good state of cultivation'. Lead and copper mining figured prominently in the economy of the area, as did slate quarrying. The woollen industry was one of the major sources of employment and only ceased being so in recent years. Under the domestic system many women in the area were kept fully occupied in knitting at home.

Further Reading:
Richard Tudor Edwards: *William Morgan*, John Jones Publishing, 1968

Talsarnau

Talsarnau is situated on the A496 between Maentwrog and Harlech. The village was built on land reclaimed from the sea. Sir John Wynn of Gwydir and Sir Hugh Myddleton were considering the reclamation of the Glaslyn estuary as early as 1625. But it was not until two centuries later that the enterprising William Maddox began a subscription fund in order to raise the money with which to build the Cob at Porthmadog, a scheme to which the poet, Shelley, also lent his support.

Today Talsarnau may appear to be a very ordinary and unexceptional village, but it is a place with at least some interesting historical and literary associations.

A mile or so from the village and quite close to the estuary is the church of Llanfihangel-y-traethau. It was here that Mari Evans, 'Y Fantell Wen' (the white robe) is buried. In the eighteenth century she founded a sect and renounced earthly things. Indeed, she went even further than that and claimed that the only marriage she would ever be prepared to enter into was with her saviour, Jesus Christ. She even went through a bizarre wedding ceremony at Llan Ffestiniog Church so that her extreme, almost sexual love, of Jesus might be recognised. She was totally convinced that by giving herself to the Son of God in this way her immortality would be ensured. When she died in 1789 her followers left the body unburied, presumably in the hope that she would miraculously rise from the dead. However, an official of the parish was empowered to issue an order for burial.

Two distinguished twentieth century personalities also lie in the remote and tranquil churchyard.

David Ormesby Gore, the fifth Earl of Harlech, is buried here. As British Ambassador in the United States during the Kennedy period, he became a close friend of the President and his family.

The novelist Richard Hughes lived at Môr Edrin, close to the church, from 1947 until his death in 1976 and, he too, is buried in the churchyard. A meticulous literary craftsman, his fictional output was fairly small, largely because of the lengthy periods of time he would spend working on each book. His best-known works are *A High Wind in Jamaica* and *The Fox in the Attic*.

Another novelist associated with the village is Gwyneth Vaughan, who was born in Talsarnau in 1852, the daughter of a miller. She wrote four Welsh language works of fiction including *Plant y Gorthrwm*.

No account of Talsarnau would be complete without mention of the remarkable maritime wanderer, David Evans, who was born at a farm called Fucheswen in 1817. He was a member of the crew of one of a number of ships which left Porthmadog on trading ventures and by the time he was twenty was Master of the Gwen Evans which up to that time was reputed to be the largest vessel built in Wales. It was involved in trade to America. Evans was even shipwrecked for a while. In 1853, he and his family decided to make their home in Wisconsin and when the Civil War broke out in 1861, he enlisted as a combatant.

For some thirty years after this, he was an employee of the United States Revenue Service, although not in a dull office-based post. He was in charge of both sail and steam vessels on the Atlantic and Pacific seaboards and later off the coast of Alaska. Evans left a fascinating account of his experiences in letters, which he wrote to a boyhood friend from Meirionnydd. Many of these are included in *Letters from America: Captain David Evans of Talsarnau 1817-1895*, edited by Lewis Lloyd, Aled Eames and Bryn Parry.

We now move forward in time to a much publicised murder case, which occurred in the village in 1952.

John Roberts, who lived at the School House, died suddenly and in suspicious circumstances. In middle age he had married Alicia Hughes, an Irish born woman. It was a second marriage for both of them and life soon began to become fraught with difficulties within the marriage. Roberts had his children living in the School House with him and when his adult daughter, Doreen, returned to Talsarnau from Birmingham, where she had been working, things deteriorated still further due to overcrowding in what was a small house. Matters were not helped by Roberts who did nothing to improve the situation. Indeed, he behaved in a negative way and even threatened to commit suicide. Not very long afterwards he was taken ill and Alicia Roberts attempted to nurse him. She made him porridge one morning but very soon afterwards he began to vomit violently. He quickly deteriorated and died. A local GP, who examined him, became suspicious and reported the death to a coroner. The doctor's concern was justified, for a report indicated that death had been due to acute arsenic poisoning. Subsequent investigations by the police revealed that Alicia Roberts had purchased amounts of arsenic from a Porthmadog chemist prior to Roberts's death.

She was arrested on suspicion of murder and, on the face of it, all the evidence appeared to be heavily against her. The eminent forensic pathologist, Dr Francis Camps, was asked to provide evidence for the defence. As a result, the prosecution case was defeated, despite putting forward what appeared at the time to be some sound evidence.

There can be little doubt that Camps was responsible for saving Alicia Roberts from being hanged, for capital punishment at that time was the ultimate penalty for murder. He claimed that due to the decomposition of John Roberts's body it was not possible to ascertain the exact cause of death with any certainty. The jury, therefore, returned an open verdict.

Trawsfynydd

Trawsfynydd is situated six miles north east of Harlech on the A470.

As in the case with so many other areas of northwest Wales, the Trawsfynydd area assumed importance during the Roman period.

Tomen y Mur is the site of a Roman military complex and is widely regarded as one of the most important sites of its kind in Britain.

The name is derived from a late eighteenth century earthwork castle built over the rampart of the Roman fort. The history of this later fortification is fairly obscure but it would seem that William Rufus campaigned here in 1095.

We know rather more about the site during the Roman period, when it was called Mur y Castell (Castle Wall), the name by which it is referred to in the *Mabinogion*.

To the best of our knowledge it was built in AD 7 or thereabouts following Agricola's campaign and would have been a wooden structure. However, it was rebuilt in stone in about AD 20 but its role as a garrison was limited after this and by the middle of the second century AD it could well have been abandoned.

We take a leap forward in time now to the sixteenth century. St John Roberts was born at Rhiwgoch in Trawsfynydd in 1577 and may have been baptised at St Madryn's Church. He was brought up as a Protestant and in 1595 went to St John's College, Oxford. He later travelled widely and while on the continent became a Catholic convert. In 1599 he attended St Benedict's Abbey at Valladolid and in the following year went to Santiago de Compostela. Having joined the Benedictines he assumed the name Fray Juan de Meiriona (Brother John of Meirionnydd). He was ordained in 1602 and returned to Britain. He was the first monk to return to the country following the dissolution of the monasteries by Henry VIII.

However, he fell foul of the authorities more than once and was fortunate to be lightly penalised with only short periods of imprisonment. He was living at a time when the plague was a widespread threat and felt great sympathy for the victims. He devoted a good deal of time caring for the sick and bringing them spiritual solace during their last days.

St John Roberts was eventually regarded as a traitor by the authorities purely because of his religious adherence. He was arrested in 1610 and faced the ultimate penalty of being hanged, drawn and quartered at Tyburn.

If Roberts was the most notable religious figure to see the light of day at Trawsfynydd then there can be no doubt as to who the foremost literary figure was.

Ellis Humphrey Evans was born at Yr Ysgwrn, a small farm, on 13th January, 1887. In his youth he established a reputation under the bardic name of Hedd Wyn. He wrote, among other things, about the young men of the area who had perished in battle during the first two years of the 1914-1918 war. One critic wrote of him:

> Hedd is a poet of promise who composes verses as easily as breathing. If he can escape the German bullets more will be heard of him.

But, in February 1917 Hedd enlisted in order to spare his younger brother Bob. He was posted to a military camp near Liverpool to serve in the Royal Welch Fusiliers. In June he was drafted to France where he underwent a monotonous period of training. In moments of respite Hedd was able to complete an awdl entitled, 'The Hero', which he was working on for submission to the committee of the National Eisteddfod to be held at Birkenhead. At the chairing ceremony Hedd Wyn's name was announced as the winning bard but no one, who crowded into the pavilion that day, had any means of knowing the terrible truth, for the bard lay dead on foreign soil.

His battalion had come under fire from German defences in the Battle of Ypres and he was one of 31,000 who were killed in the carnage. The notoriously unfeeling General Haig, speaking in a blinkered military context referred to it as 'a fine day's work'.

A memorial statue of Hedd Wyn was erected in the village depicting him not as a soldier but as a shepherd. On it the following lines are inscribed:

Ei aberth nid a heibio – ei wyneb
  Annwyl nid a'n ango',
Er i'r Almaen ystaenio
Ei dwrn dur yn ei waed o.

(His sacrifice will not be in vain/his dear face will not be forgotten/although Germany has stained/her iron fist with his blood).

We now move into the next decade when the river Prysor was diverted and harnessed into the formation of a manmade lake, on the eastern side of which the nuclear power station was later built.

Earlier on Trawsfynydd had achieved prominence on the railway map of Wales when, in 1882, the thirty two mile long Great Western Line from Blaenau Ffestiniog to Bala opened.

Work on the construction of the railway took four years but in 1961 operations ceased as a result of the decision to begin work on Llyn Celyn, on ground through which the line ran.

The route cut through some of the most difficult upland areas of Meirionnydd and a few months after it opened a passenger train was trapped in snowdrifts near Carn Bryncelyn and the driver, fireman, guard and passengers were forced to bed down for the night there. The last train to use the line ran on 22nd January, 1961. The rails were removed and parts of the track used to build the present road between Trawsfynydd and Bala.

The lake, which is three miles in length, was formed in order to drive a hydroelectric power station six hundred feet below in the Maentwrog valley. The land belonging to twenty five farms was affected by the flooding.

Sir Basil Spence, who also designed the new cathedral at Coventry, designed the nuclear power station. Building work began in 1959 and it was to employ two thousand people. Understandably, there was intense controversy about the location of what some regarded as a monstrosity within a national park.

It was the first inland nuclear power station in Britain and was only decommissioned in the last few years.

Trefriw

Trefriw is situated on the banks of the river Conwy, five miles north of Betws-y-coed on the B5106.

St Rhychwyn Church has been referred to as the oldest in Wales. It is built on the site where it is thought Rhychwyn established a place of worship in the sixth century.

According to popular folklore, the wife of Prince Llywelyn, who was the daughter of none other than King John, was fatigued by the walk she had to make uphill to the church. So, her very considerate husband had St Mary's Church built for her in Trefriw. They are both depicted in a stained glass window there.

In the fourth century the Roman XX Legion was garrisoned at Caerhun, the fortress that controlled both the Conwy Valley and Caernarfon. They carried out extensive sulphur mining operations and, in the process, discovered the beneficial value of the minerals and as W. Bezant Lowe writes:

> . . . it is probable that the Trefriw Chalybeate Wells were in existence in those early days; but in any case they date back several hundred years.

The spring can be traced to a cave at the foot of the hill known as Allt Cae Coch. It seems that mining activity in the eighteenth century resulted in the entrance to the cave becoming blocked. It was only in 1833 that it was reopened. It was not very long before the healing qualities of the water became well known and, as a result, people with a range of afflictions visited the spa. In 1863, Lord Willoughby de Eresby of Gwydir erected, at his own expense, the first bathhouse. Within ten years the enterprise was leased to a local company and they erected the present pump house. During the next forty years a new pump room was added together with a suite of baths.

In the Victorian period visitors travelled to the well by boat from Conwy and Deganwy with hundreds arriving each week in the summer season. Accommodation was provided at Trefriw.

Something of the appeal of the spa is conveyed in the following poem. Although lacking in literary quality, it remains an interesting item relating to the social history of Trefriw.

In Praise of Trefriw Waters and Baths

To Trefriw Wells a lady came,
Her nerves all shattered, old and lame,
Her joy of life and spirit spent
Her days were one long lament
Against the wretched motor man
Who knocked her down within a span.
This shocked her nerves, caused sleeplessness
The broken arm gave hopelessness
With bruises, cuts and all contusions
She listened to her friends' effusions
To join them in the loveliest spot
That lovely nature, ere begot
To drink the water from the well
Which pain and anguish quickly quell.
She came, she drank, the bath she tried
And sleep returned so long denied.
Had she the ready writers flow
This wondrous cure all men should know.

When the National Health Service came into being in the nineteen forties those with certain physical afflictions no longer sought the benefit of hydrotherapy. As a result, the spa went into decline and was eventually abandoned. However, after a time it was purchased by a local family who were quick to realise its potential in terms of tourism. Today you can pay a visit and, with the aid of a push button audio guide, capture at least something of the atmosphere of the spa in Victorian and Edwardian times. The present building also incorporates a tearoom and natural beauty salon.

There are three lakes situated within a fairly close radius of Trefriw. Cowlyd is the deepest, not only in Snowdonia, but indeed the whole of northern Wales and provides Colwyn Bay and Conwy with their water supply.

There are myths and legends associated with many of the lakes of Wales and Cowlyd is no exception. Indeed, we find a reference to it in the *Mabinogion*. Culhwch is given certain tasks to perform before he can be granted consent to marry Olwen, the daughter of Ysbyddadan. One of these involved the search for Mabon. He relies on the wisdom and knowledge of the creatures of the wild to enable him to pursue the quest, among them being 'the owl of Cwm Cowlyd'.

> They came to a place where the Owl of Cwm Cawlwyd was. 'Owl of Cwm Cawlwyd, here are Arthur's messengers. Knowest thou aught of Mabon son of Modron, who was taken away from his mother when three nights old?' 'If I knew it, I would tell it. When first I came hither, the great valley you see was a wooded glen, and a race of men came thereto and it was laid waste. And the second wood grew therein, and this wood is the third. And as for me, why! the roots of my wings are mere stumps. From that day to this I have heard naught of the man you are asking after. Nevertheless I will be guide to Arthur's messengers until you come to the place where is the oldest creature that is in the world, and he that has fared farthest afield, the Eagle of Gwernabwy.

Richard James bequeathed Llyn Crafnant in order to provide Llanrwst with its water supply. It is a mecca for anglers and there is a regular restocking scheme. The maximum depth of the lake has been measured at seventy one feet.

The third lake is Geirionnydd, another favourite spot for visitors. Along the east shore runs the possible route of Sarn Helen, the Roman road from north to south Wales.

It is also of some interest in a cultural context. Ieuan Glan Geirionnydd (1795-1855) was born, fairly close to the lake. For a time, he was the curate of Trefriw and composed poems and hymns.

David Francis (1865-1929) was frequently referred to as 'the blind harpist of Meirion'. He took part in many eisteddfodau, some of which were held only a few hundred yards away from the lake.

The bard, Gwilym Cowlyd (1828-1902), was born at Trefriw and became a printer and bookseller. He was a nephew of Ieuan Glan Geirionnydd and made a significant contribution to the work, which was started by his uncle.

Gwilym Cowlyd is chiefly remembered today because of his endeavour to establish a bardic institution, which he felt, would rival the well established Gorsedd Beirdd Ynys Prydain, a society of poets, musicians and other representatives of the best in the culture of the region at that time, which had been founded by Iolo Morgannwg in 1792. Gwilym called his assembly 'Arwest Glan Geirionnydd' and it met annually between 1865 and 1890 close to the lake. Initially it was a success but by 1900 it had few supporters. He died a disappointed man having been declared bankrupt during the final years of his life.

In the no doubt genuine and well intentioned belief that the sixth century poet, Taliesin, was born close to the lake, Lord Willoughby de Eresby of Gwydir, was instrumental in the erection of a monument to perpetuate his memory. However, there does not, to my knowledge, appear to be any evidence at all to link the bard to this corner of northern Wales.

No account of Trefriw would be complete without a look at the contribution of the woollen industry to its social history. The mill still flourishes and attracts many visitors each year. It was originally a 'pandy' or fulling mill to which local people brought their cloth to be washed and shrunk. The soft water of Afon Crafnant was used to wash the cloth and drive two water wheels.

Thomas Williams of Pentrefoelas was responsible for the establishment of the present mill. He came to take the waters in the village and quickly realised the potential of the mill alongside the Afon Crafnant. He extended the buildings and installed an overshot wheel, thirty six feet in diameter, to drive machines called 'billies' and 'jennies' for making woollen yarn and also a second wheel seven feet in diameter for driving the 'pandy' mill for fulling the cloth woven on hand looms.

Further down the river other trades and industries relied on water – a smithy, a sawmill and a flour mill. Early in the nineteenth century a forge had been established manufacturing hammers and other tools for the use of quarry workers. It employed some twenty men.

According to one source, Trefriw was at one time regarded as a major Welsh inland port. General merchandise was transported up the river Conwy from the coast and boats returned with ore, slate and timber on board.

Ysbyty Ifan

Ysbyty Ifan is situated on the B4407 between Pentrefoelas and Llan Ffestiniog.

This small and attractive village of grey stoned houses in the shadow of the vast hinterland area known as the Migneint has a distinctive history.

It evolved as a result of the initiation of the Knights of St John of Jerusalem. In the late Middle Ages the Order exemplified an important ideal at a time when there was considerable conflict between Christians and Saracens in the Holy Land. The Order came into being following the first Crusade and the entry of the Christian Knights into Jerusalem in the summer of 1099, following a protracted siege. Henceforth, the day on which this triumph occurred became the anniversary of the founding of the Knights of St John. Soon afterwards they founded a hospice where the needs of the sick and the poor could be met.

Pope Paschal II issued a bill, which formalised the Order in 1113, and, as a result, the duties became both holy and secular. Military duties were minimalised. As time went by they acquired both land and wealth and hospices were established in various parts of Europe.

The first Welsh hospice was at Slebech in Pembrokeshire. This was during a period when Wales and England were independent countries and the Welsh Princes were reluctant to recognise the Order.

When Giraldus Cambrensis was accompanying Archbishop Baldwin on a recruiting campaign for the Crusaders in 1188 they celebrated mass at St Asaph Cathedral. This may well have resulted in the donation of land by Ifan ap Rhys of Plas Iolyn expressly for a hospice at Ysbyty Ifan. This was dedicated to St John the Baptist and would have been constructed of wood. It may well have been destroyed by fire during Owain Glyndŵr's uprising in 1400.

In the thirteenth century it is thought that the Order was in receipt of a good deal of wealth and to add to this they acquired a church and mill at Penmachno as well as further properties.

The village was conveniently situated on a traveller's route close to the old Roman road from the Conwy Valley to the English border.

In an ode, which is thought to have been compared in the mid-fourteenth century addressed to a nobleman, an interesting comparison is made between his generosity and that provided by the hospice:

St John's great hospice feeds not more
Than Rhys ap Tywyn's bounteous store.

Ysbyty Ifan was the administrative centre for the collection of dues from the estates. Voluntary contributions for the whole of Gwynedd were also collected here.

The main function of the hospice was the provision of food and shelter but there is no evidence that it was anything like what we envisage when we think of hospices today.

We know very little about the men who served the hospice. But we do know that a man named Ednyfed was in charge in the late eleventh century. There appears to be some evidence to suggest that he was in receipt of compensation for damage inflicted on the building by soldiers of Edward I during his conquest of Wales.

The knights were granted the privilege of administering the law within their lands. The effect of this was important for it led to a sanctuary being created in this small community.

Following the Glyndŵr rebellion, law and order was flaunted in parts of northern Wales and many crimes, including murder, occurred. Sir John Wynn of Gwydir wrote:

. . . there was continually fostered a wasps' nest, which troubled the hole countrey, I mean a lordship belonging to St Johns of Jerusalmen, called Spytty Jevan, a large thing; which had privilege of sanctuary. This peculiar jurisdiction, not governed by the King's Lawes, became a receptacle of thieves and murtherers, who safely being warranted there by law, made the place thoroughly peopled. Noe spot within twenty miles was safe from their incursions and roberies, and what they got within their limits was their owne . . . In this estate stood the hundred of Nantconway, when

Meredith removed his dwelling thither . . . in the beginning of King Henry the Seventh his time'.

It was inevitable that in these circumstances the reputation of the hospice became tarnished and it became well known that it was a place where the law could be defied.

Meredudd ap Ifan was determined to rid the area of criminals and his efforts met with success. It is still believed by some historians that he did not take them into captivity but put pressure on them to flee. It seems that they then transferred their troublemaking to the Dinas Mawddwy area where they became known at Gwylliaid Cochion Mawddwy (The Red Bandits).

When the Tudors came to the throne the life of the Order was short-lived. They had obtained their privileges from the Church of Rome and the wealth and power, which they represented, posed a threat to a rapidly changing world. The Order was dissolved and the properties seized by the Crown.

The Order is commemorated in a stained glass window in St John's Church in the village. The present building dates from 1858 and certainly deserves a visit.

Here you will discover some interesting effigies. Included among these is one in memory of Rhys Fawr ap Meredydd, which probably dates from 1483. He is depicted in a fine suit of armour, as he was thought to have been the standard bearer to Henry VII at the Battle of Bosworth. His son, who was a chaplain to Cardinal Wolsey, is also commemorated.

Moving forward to the nineteenth century we find an unexpected historical link with America, for the great-grandmother of Abraham Lincoln was born in a grey stoned farmhouse, Bryn Gwyn. Ellen Morys was the daughter of John Morys and lived there until her emigration to the United States in the early eighteenth century. Soon after her arrival in the New World she met and married Cadwaladar Evans, who hailed from the Penllyn area. Their daughter, Sara, married John Hanks from Virginia. They, in turn, gave birth to a daughter, Nancy, and she married into the Lincoln family.

A further well-known American also has a link with Ysbyty Ifan but, this time, a well-known film star. In 1978, a second screen adaptation of Emlyn Williams' play, *The Corn is Green*, was filmed largely on location in the village. Katherine Hepburn played the part of the schoolteacher, Miss Moffatt.